TABERNACLE OF LIES

Memoirs of Innocence Lost
BOOK 1

BY FERRON P. WILEY

Debie
Thank you for
taking the time to
Read my Story

Much Love
Ferron P. Wiley

PROLOGUE

Houston Texas 2019

I've been trying to write this story for nearly 15 years now. Distractions are a bitch. Depression can be a major distraction I guess. I am not in any kind of physical turmoil, I have a consistent income, and as far as I know, I am reasonably healthy and I have some really great friends. All anyone could really ask for really. Yet there is this nagging sense that there is supposed to be more. Why can't I ever just be fucking content? I've heard people say a number of times you just need to focus on what you do have and not so much on what you think you don't have. But when you're a person that spends most of their time living inside your own head that can be difficult. I have never been much of a go-getter. I have always just kind of let life happen and went with it. Less disappointment that way I've always thought. At 50 years old now, I have definitely slowed down quite a bit and have found time again to reflect.

Outside of having never fallen in love, there aren't a lot of things in my life that I wanted to do that I haven't done, and today I am not sure that experience is all that everyone makes it out to be. Let me be clear, I believe being in love means, that the love you have for a person is authentically being reciprocated. They want you as much as you want them. So while I have perhaps loved, and been loved, I have not ever been in love. Well not since my very first boyfriend but does that really count when you don't really know what love is? I certainly have not relished the feeling of chasing after things I could never actually attain. So over the years, I learned to lean toward things that provided me more immediate gratification. As I look back over and reflect on my life, I think I probably could have used a lot more therapy, but it just wasn't something I could afford, and of course, the positive returns that therapeutic investments may provide are never immediate. At least never immediate enough.

I thought to myself after all this time what does my life have to show for itself, what will be my legacy, will I have one at all? Does any of it even matter? Today, I guess I decided. Yes, my life matters. My story should be told. I should be the one to tell it since I am the only one it's important enough to to tell it. More than likely no one else will.

Just because of the way some movies I've seen approach storytelling, I always thought that you should start at the good part, start at the moment of triumph and then go back to all the horrible, tragic shit to show how you made it to said triumph. Then, cue the orchestra, release the confetti, pan into the distance from the final kiss and roll the credits, so everybody can go home feeling good. My story, however, seems to be filled with more defeat than triumph so it's hard to know where to begin. So, I guess I'll begin with the moment that at least I thought was going to be most triumphant. The moment that I thought was going to put me back in the good graces of God, my family and subsequently would make me the whole person I wanted to be. I was wrong, again as usual, but here we go anyway.

CHAPTER 1

Dallas Texas 2005

I present to you the body of Faith Alive Church, here in Dallas Texas, Minister Ferron P. Wiley. A servant to the body of Christ. Apostle Allen E. Burns words were uttered in the course of this ministerial installment service. I began to weep in the presence of God as the applause of this small congregation filled the room where four others and I had been officially licensed as ministers in this radically inclusive church. I had become overwhelmed with emotion. I was humbled by the thoughts of God's awesome power.

"God, this is what I have desired my entire life." I thought to myself. "How did I get here? You have done what I thought would never ever happen. After all the things I had gone through in my life, all the crap that my life had touched."

" My God, I had only been to Bible school for two weeks and I couldn't really pay attention then. How could you see fit for me to stand up in front of anyone and be recognized as... Minister?"

" I don't remember a time when I have ever felt closer to you. There were glimpses, but thinking back and connecting the dots I can see the image of your hand upon my life from the very beginning."

Rochester New, York 1973

Growing up in Rochester New York from what I remember was not an overall unpleasant experience. It was generally a friendly city for the most part. Rochester was a technology town and home two well-known companies like Kodak, Xerox, Bausch & Lomb as well as educational establishments like the University of Rochester and the Rochester Institute of Technology. I was born in Toms River New Jersey on August 14th, 1968, just a few months after Martin Luther King was assassinated. Mom told me once she remembered seeing news coverage of the continued aftermath of his death while she was in the hospital. I was the youngest of three when our family moved to Rochester when I was around 1 year old. There's not too much to say about those very early years for obvious reasons but as I recall I had a family that loved me. I just remember being a little boy exploring life and my love and talent for music. I remember we had an old electric organ. it was small enough to fit in me and my brother's bedroom, but I would spend so much time driving everyone nuts playing it, it was eventually moved to the attic. Later, I was being referred to by my Dad as the Phantom of the Opera as mysterious music would emanate from the eaves of the house.

My father was a very fair-skinned black man. Often, people mistook him for being white. He was a former Navy pilot and corporate executive for the Xerox Corporation. He was stationed at the Naval Base in Lakehurst New Jersey from what I understand until somewhere around my birth and his discharge from active duty in the Navy. I remember him dropping us off at Aenon Baptist Church for Sunday school. Sometimes my sister, my brother and I would stay for the Sunday service, other times Dad would come and pick us up before it started. After a while, there was a time that we didn't go to church at all. I do remember though in later years Dad spent Sunday afternoons after Church having family bible studies with us, he was brilliantly intelligent. I remember days when he would instruct us to give speeches in front of the family. He said it was important for us to learn how to talk to people with confidence.

I remember on nice days he would take me out to the street in front of our house and we would play tennis together. As with most things in life, there was also a very dark side to my father. He was a very stoic, stern, angry and at times explosive man. He was difficult to read sometimes and other times I think he was so angry that he must have thought he needed to just be emotionless as not to seriously harm anyone. I remember him disappearing in his home office a lot, not coming out for hours. This happened on one of my birthdays once. I thought it was my fault that he didn't want to come out. I often didn't know how to talk to him, or if I should, as there was always the chance of my head being bitten off.

My Mother was a sing-song, caring, loving, nurturing woman always dedicated to the health and unity of our family. She was June Cleaver, Martha Stewart and Claire Huxtable all rolled into one. I remember her coming to a place in her life that she decided to leave her beauty and modeling career to be at home with her family. She aggressively moved into what she believed was her God-ordained role as a wife and mother. She always stepped out taking unpopular paths if she believed God was leading her, especially when it came to healthy eating or child-rearing. There were slow changes for us and our diets at first. A little wheat germ in the morning cereal, which I could covertly shake to the bottom of the bowl before adding milk. There was wheat toast instead of white. There were also times when I felt like we were the damn Swiss Family Robinson and tree bark was the main course. Nonetheless, my mother was an amazing cook. She made her way through finding the appropriate balances for us, but not compromising for anything the direction she believed God was leading her. Ultimately I know she loved us even though it took some time for our taste buds to come into agreement. It was her spirit that charged me up and inspired me to move forward to try new things in my own life. She was committed to God, her husband, and her children, and she was a testimony of what mothers and wives can be to their families.

Fear of disappointing her at the same time often paralyzed me.

I was the youngest of three children but the only biological child to my father. We were all aware of my mother's previous marriage but we lived as a family. The terms step-dad or step-brother or sister were never used. My sister and my brother were 6 and 5 years ahead of me respectively. For the most part, we got along pretty well. We had minor conflicts that always seemed major at the time, but because of our age difference, I often felt disconnected from both of them. My Sister used to let me hang out with her and her different girlfriends and boyfriends sometimes, she even let me come to some of the parties she threw. I think however that when she discovered that I was not mature enough or perhaps mature beyond my years, to keep my mouth shut about certain events that transpired, being included on her outings quickly came to an end.

My Brother and I seemed to be closer when we were younger, but once he hit adolescence he was off and running. He had a life with sports and friends and he was gone a lot.

I had friends to play with that I spent most of my summer days, many until the sun went down. We were kids that still played outside as video games yet were still predominantly big machines found only in bowling alleys or arcades. Cable TV was only fifteen extra channels of other local stations around the state. We would roleplay and reenact scenes from popular Science Fiction TV shows and movies of the day, Star Trek, Space 1999, Star Wars and Battlestar Galactica. Whenever we played I would always pick the character that could shape-shift. I always liked the idea of being able to become something or someone else.

I never did like school very much and found myself in trouble often, nothing too major early on, just mischief. I remember kindergarten pretty vividly. I guess I remember this because it was the first and last time I ever brought a boy I liked home. I even remember his name, Chris. He was the cutest thing and he must have thought I was too because he followed me all the way home. When we got there, my mom came to the door and asked in her sing-song voice,
Who is this?
Dis Chris. I said.
Chris, does your mother know that you're here? My mother asked.
Chris shrugged his shoulders.
"Can we play Mommy?" I asked.
Mom brought us both into the house and sat us in the patterned, forest green, vinyl coated chairs at the kitchen table.
"Are you guys hungry?" She asked while she removed an information card from Chris's jacket.
"Ye-e-e-s." We replied simultaneously.
"Do you like peanut butter and jelly Chris?" Mom asked.
"Yes ma'am I do," Chris said, smiling his missing teeth.
My mother proceeded to fix us both a peanut butter and jelly sandwich and left us to eat while she went to call Chris's mother at the number she retrieved from the card on his jacket.

Curious to me, Chris had opened up his peanut butter and jelly sandwich and asked me, "Do you have any smooth peanut butter?"

"I don't think so", I said.

To my amazement, Chris started picking all the peanuts out of his sandwich.

"What are you doing?" I asked.

"I don't like the nuts," Chris replied.

"Well I got a hold of your mother," Mom said coming back into the room.

She looked down and saw Chris's sandwich torn to bits and she offered him something else to eat.

I was mortified. I didn't realize it then, but this experience would jade me for many relationships to come. Here was this fine young boy who naturally and without any inhibition followed me home. After presenting him to my mother and laying out the red carpet for him, he embarrasses me in front of her by picking over the meal she prepared for him. They will never get in this easily again!

Chris's mother arrived sometime later. I can't say that I didn't harbor a little petty satisfaction inside seeing his mom shake him around and scold him on the way to her car for not coming directly home.

I was aware of my attraction to my own gender at a very young age. I can't say I knew exactly what it was at the time but during the years before the peanut butter sandwich incident, I had a pretty peaceful existence with my imaginary friend. He was a fireman who came home from firefighting at night and got into bed with me. His name was Steve. Stories may conflict but I don't really ever recall giving Mom and Dad much trouble going to bed at night.

I actually started exploring sex with boys in first grade. His name I don't recall because I think it was just what it was, ol' dirty sex. Anyway, we went into the coatroom and closed the door. There we sat in the dark room together and he told me to say the word "pussy" three times real fast, over and over.

"Pussy Pussy Pussy," we said, and then, we just left. Afterward, I felt dirty and ashamed but strangely exhilarated as well.

I always get a chuckle out of the opening sequence of that popular TV show Will & Grace when Jack and Karen are shown bouncing their bellies together because that exactly depicts my first physical sexual contact with another male. We raised up our shirts and pressed our bellies together and called it social studies. Thereafter whenever we were together, one of us would always say to the other, let's have social studies.

I remember feeling warm and funny inside whenever I would see Mr.Taylor. He was the Vice-Principal and disciplinarian of John Spencer Elementary School #16 in the 19th Ward district of Rochester New York. He was a tall black man with a salt and pepper afro and mustache. His appearance sort of puts you in the mind of popular former CBN broadcasting 700 Club co-host, Ben Kinchlow. Mr. Taylor was very masculine and commanded respect. Some days I would get into trouble just to be sent to his office. One day I had drawn a pair of big titts on my school papers and turned them into the teacher, knowing I would immediately be sent to see Mr. Taylor. Mr. Taylor obviously had had enough of my behavior, so he decided to step up his intervention.

He was taking me home to my mother. I was terrified of having to be accountable to my mother but exhilarated at the same time that I was getting to sit so close to him in his car for the whole ride home. I think I was suspended for the rest of the day and I had to apologize to the teacher. At the time though, it was worth it to me. Of course, I came to my senses and realized that Mr. Taylor's patience was wearing thin with me. I couldn't bear the thought of him not liking me and I didn't want to get kicked out of school. So, I backed off. At least I would be able to admire him from afar.

Truth be told, I do not remember much about second grade other than a few fights with older boys trying to pick on me and steal my stuff. I landed a few good shin kicks with my patent leather hard heeled shoes and the bullies pretty much left me alone after that. I also had taken it upon myself to initiate piano lessons with the school music teacher, Mrs. Schicholi- Pratt. She told me that if I wanted to learn then I would have to come in early on Tuesdays for my lesson. I did, but the lessons were short-lived because Mrs. Schicholi- Pratt soon moved away with Mr. Pratt, her newly wedded husband.

I remember chasing Skippy the ice cream man down the street with my 50 cents for my Bomb Pop. I remember my sister's cakes she made in her Suzy Homemaker Oven. I remember climbing through a hole in my bedroom wall and trying to slide down the banister on the staircase on the other side. The hole was there because the house caught on fire at Christmas time that past year. I remember my big brother being in Boy Scouts and him getting to stay up a little past bedtime on nights he had meetings. My brother and I shared a room and I was always in bed by the time he came back.

Once there was a family pool night sponsored at school #44. The whole family went. I don't recall being able to swim at that time but I've never been afraid of the water. When it was time to go we all went into the locker room to change back into dry things. I started undressing. Mom brought a robe for me to put on. As I was slipping into the robe, Dad came from behind and snatched it off of me. I just stood there naked and Mom finish dressing me in my clothes. When we got home,

Dad came into our bedroom and told us to take off our clothes. We did because there was never a time when it was ok to disobey Dad. Dad did the same. We were all naked in the room. He told us to join hands and the three of us danced around in a circle together, naked. "See, he's looking at yours, you're looking at mine we all got one ain't nothing wrong with being naked." He exhorted.

Then, we all got dressed, and that was it. I was not sure at the time what the exact point of this fun lesson was, but it sure did lower my inhibitions about a lot of things. Like one day when one of my uncles we visited, was giving us a tour through his house, I turned to him out of the blue, in front of everyone and inquisitively blurted out,

"Do you have a penis?"

There was one day that I remember that I wanted to spend the day with my Dad. I don't remember why exactly it was so important, but I remember begging my Dad not to go to work that day and stay with me, Mom had to hold me back from going after him toward the car and I fell out in a tantrum in the driveway when he drove away.

There were some quiet years for me following. I was busy growing up. I used to like catching bees in a mayonnaise jar that I had poked holes in the top of for them to breathe. I would try to break my own record of how many bees I could catch in one jar. I think I got up to 13. At the end of the day when the sun was setting, I would set them free by just removing the cap. I would watch them fly one by one up, up and up in a circle. I deduced that since they had been in captivity for so long that they had conformed into a certain pattern of movement, going round and round as if they were still trying to reach the top of the jar. It wouldn't be until much later in my life that I actually grasp the principle of what I was seeing.

We moved out to the suburbs in Pittsville Ponds New York, a life change to some degree. I had to change schools and attended third grade in the Weighton school district. I think it was the closest school to our new home that would accept me at the time. I think Mom and Dad had to lie and say we were still residing at our old address to get me in. I think they couldn't get me into Pittsville Ponds schools because we had not established residency for a year yet. Mom would drop me off at school and she taught me how to catch public transportation home. The first day of riding the bus home though I failed the test. I had just missed the bus within seconds. A man who saw me running for the bus and my dismay over missing it pulled up and offered me a ride. Not wanting to disappoint my mother, I jumped into the car and we sped off after the bus. Eventually, we passed the bus at the next stop and he pulled in front letting me out. I got on the bus and rode the rest of the way home but little did I know that Mom had been watching from across the street in front of the school to make sure I made it on the bus that day and had seen and followed the entire incident from start to finish. When she walked through the front door I recognized the look on her face. Instead of her being filled with congratulations, "you made it home on your own baby", she looked frazzled and angry.

"What's wrong Mommy?" I asked.

Pausing to gain her composure, she replied,

"Who was that you got in the car with?"

"Um... I don't know, he helped me catch the bus cuz I missed it." I said.

She was breathing heavily and looked like she was going to cry.

"Don't choo NEVER, get in nobody's car and you don't know who they are!! Do you hear me?!!

I felt horrible, I knew I had let her down. I'm sorry Mommy, I won't do it again.

A year or so went by and I was able to be enrolled in Pittsville Ponds schools. I remember Dad taking me to the new school for enrollment. It was a very tall building made of brick and it had large white pillars in front. To me, it looked like a university campus compared to the other schools I had attended. I began 4th grade at Pittsville Ponds Elementary School. Suddenly I was in an environment that was occupied predominantly by white people. I'd learn to adjust quickly, however. I was not aware of any overt racism other than the black students that were bused into the suburban school where I attended were always referred to as "the city kids" by teachers and students alike. I was often grouped with the city kids even though I lived in the district where the school was. Once, a teacher quibbled with me because I was not lining up with the "city kids" to get on the "city bus" back to the "city."

I remember feeling like an outsider to everyone, not only for the color of my skin but also the lack thereof. I was light-skinned in all aspects of my life. I didn't really identify with most black people because I wasn't living the life of black people or so I thought. I had already been conditioned to think I was better because of where I lived. I certainly didn't identify with white people because I wasn't one. I immediately became isolated and started doing poorly in school. I made friends with outcasts as I thought I was one as well. Todd Laycock; I think I'm just gonna let that go. Todd was a curly red-headed obnoxious kid who as it turned out was very insecure and couldn't stand to be away from home for very long. Luckily he lived within walking distance from the school. He turned out to be my only friend through Elementary School. Todd and I spent lots of time together over each other's house. Well, mostly at his house because the first time he came over to spend the night at my house, he woke up in the middle of the night crying because he was homesick. We had to call his Dad to come to get him. I decided that my weekend wouldn't be ruined, I would go stay over his house. Strangely enough, while I was there we, of course, started having conversations that young boys often do, about sex. He wanted to know if I ever had messed around with a girl and how far I'd gotten.

He started bragging about the things he had done, but I didn't believe him. But now I was starting to feel comfortable with Todd so I told him some things about how I feel about boys and how it made me feel when I thought about them or when I was near them.

" Oh my God, you mess around with boys?!"

"SHHH!" I said.

"Well, anytime you're ready, let me know, Todd said.

I was stunned. I had never officially been hit on before. I felt all warm and wanted inside. Todd rolled over and went to sleep. I laid there basking in the afterglow and we hadn't even touched each other. I never did anything with Todd, I was still too afraid to try. Not ready as they say. And what if we got caught?

Todd moved away a year or so later, I really felt a sense of loss. I don't remember the last time I saw him.

Fifth and sixth grade we're kind of a blur, but I remember piano lessons with Mr. Gallows. Mr. Gallows was my theory teacher at the Hochstein School of Music. My parents decided to invest in my musical abilities. I imagine Hochstein was very expensive, however. so within a year, Mr. Gallows was giving private lessons to my mother and I at home.

Around this time I remember Mom becoming a born again Christian and started going to church. I remember my Grandmother on Dad's side coming to visit us. I remember becoming a Cub Scout, a Weblo and a boy scout. I earned my cooking badge, my sewing badge, and my interior-design while camping badge. Yaaass!

Truth be told I wasn't really down for being a scout. Yeah, I believed in the things they stood for but all that hoofing around, hiking and climbing, No thank you. "Y'all go ahead they'll be a nice meal waiting for you when you get back!" I would say. The Father and Son outings were always a disaster for me. By the time I reached Junior High School, I just stopped going to the meetings altogether. I would just hang out in the Village of Pittsville Ponds reading comic books and buying candy to eat, or stealing it when I didn't have any money. I hung out at the library and at the part of the Erie Canal that ran through our town, much of the time just looking for someone to talk to.

When it got to be time for me to be coming home from Scout meeting, I just went home and went to my room to pretend to do my homework, if it wasn't my day to clean the kitchen or something.

My connection with my family was slipping. I was even becoming aggressive at school. Not really though. I was just trying to scare that little stuck-up bitch Karen Moskowitz that sat in front of me in class. She kinda looked like Liza Minnelli, with hair like Marcie. You know. Marcie. Peppermint Patty's lesbian lover from the Peanuts cartoons? I didn't even touch her when she made some kind of crazy remark to me under her breath so I jumped up and tipped over my desk and laid on some drama when Mrs. Sagenberg put me in a bear hug and escorted me out of the classroom. I spent a good portion of the day in Miss Clark, the school counselor's office while she peered over the top of her glasses like Sally Jesse Raphael did when she was being judgmental.
"What happened in there?" She asked.
"She pissed me off!" I replied angrily.
"Is that how you normally respond when you're pissed off?"

"No," I said sarcastically. My bad attitude was increasing.

"So what made you get out of control today?"

"I wasn't out of control, if I was out of control, you all would still be trying to pull me off of her."

"Did you want to hurt her?"

"No?"

"Are you hurting inside?" She inquired, placing her hands over her chest and tilting her head slightly to one side.

"No! Look, I'm just tired of her saying mean stuff to me!"

"Do you think you're going to be able to go back into class when you calm down?"

"I am calm," I said scowling at her.

"I'm going to go see how things are in the classroom, can you stay here till I get back?"

"Yes."

After she left the room I saw Little Miss Moskowitz walking in the hallway coming from the restroom on her way back to class. She passed by the doorway of the counselor's office and then double-backed. Whispering to me through the doorway she said, "I'm sooo sorry, I didn't mean to upset you." I nodded my head to her in acknowledgment and she went back to class.

"Bitch!" I thought to myself.

When I got back to class the room was silent. I just went back to my desk feeling a little self-satisfied that I had accomplished my goal. I often wondered though if before I returned, Miss Clark had instructed the class to be patient with me and not to upset my inner angry black man.

CHAPTER 2

Junior High School. It was filled with new faces, new friends, new liberties and a new me, so I thought. We had gone home for summer vacation after 6th grade and came back to a new school and some kind of sexual revolution that I did not receive the memo for. Girls were popping out in places they weren't just 4 months ago. And boys were just popping out everywhere they possibly could. Walking the halls sometimes was like what I imagined porn to be like. Girls I had made finger paint murals with and boys I had built forts with on the playground within just the last year were pressed against each other on lockers in heated and braces and making out. I wasn't sure what to make of it all, except that it seemed to be the thing to do. I wondered when I would get a chance to do those things. I wasn't ready to think about sex at my age anyway, let alone explore my own personal desires. But I did not want to feel like the outsider I was in elementary school. So I ended up sticking with what I knew, utilizing the same formula because I didn't know what else to do. So I joined the band of misfits, geeks, athletically challenged intellectuals... The Nerds.

Jim, Rick, Craig and I hung out all the time. Jim was a tall, oddly shaped, greaseball looking white kid with acne only a mother could love. He was obsessed with playing Dungeons and Dragons. Outside of that, and us, he was pretty antisocial. Rick was Jim's sidekick, an even grease-ball-ier disheveled looking white kid with braces that didn't seem to be working at all. His industrial strength prescription lenses only cooperated to make the whole nerd ensemble complete. Craig was actually kind of cool to me. He wasn't the prettiest button on the shirt, but he was black and he had memorized Rapper's Delight to the tee. He taught it to the rest of us and every day at lunch we would pound on the table to make a beat and trade off reciting the song's verses. Craig and I, of course, hit it off the best. We were two suburban black kids "not living the black life" but I still felt like Craig was closer to it than I was. He knew how to rap. Craig filled a void of friendship that I had lost in Todd and it wasn't long before he started spending nights over on weekends.

Craig was a Sci-Fi buff too and we spent hours playing in my room. In our imaginations, we converted my lower bunk bed into the cockpit of our spaceship. They're laid on our backs we used the bottom of the top bunk as a control panel and old chairs placed in front of us as thruster and steering mechanisms. I often played a 33 RPM record of the Star Wars soundtrack that I signed out from the library on my record player for background music.

Suddenly, a Dicrazonite meteor struck the side of the ship causing the hull Integrity to be compromised. We were losing oxygen and running out of time. The ship had been knocked off course and we were headed for a planet's acidic atmosphere that would surely burn us alive. Captain Craig had determined that the polymer material in our space suits was similar to what was used in building the ship's hull. If he acted fast he might be able to find a way to repair the hull damage and buy us some time to get the ship back on course. Captain Craig feverishly tore his space suit from his body. He quickly leaned over to me put his mouth to mine and took a breath of air from my lungs and proceeded to try and repair the hull damage while I tried to steer the ship away from the planet. Our velocity was increasing and oxygen was down to 40%. Captain Craig was running out of air and it seemed as though he wasn't going to have enough material to finish the job. He threw himself on top of me, putting his lips to mine and taking another few breaths. Then he freed himself from the remainder of his spacesuit so he would have more polymer material to seal the hole. A few more grunts and angry blast with his laser soldering gun and he was done. Yes! Captain Craig fell back on top of me for one more breathing treatment before I was able to restore our oxygen levels back to normal. I was able to bring the thermal boosters back online and steer the ship out of destructions path. Captain Craig was regaining his breath.

I, was fucking on fire…

Craig was just lying there next to me with nothing on but socks, he had kissed me three times now. I was paralyzed. Endorphins were firing like 12 fourth of Julys. I didn't know what to do. I knew what I wanted to do, but I didn't know how.
"You ever jerk off before?" Craig asked, still breathing heavily.
"What's that?" I asked.
Craig was hairy down there already and I wasn't. He had become erect and simultaneously he touched himself making motions and deep breathing noises. The bed started to creak. His dick was huge.
"Quiet Man, my parents are just in the next room! I forcefully whispered. I was scared of getting caught but I didn't want it to end.

He just kept going... going... and going until...
"Fuck, yeeaah!".
I had never seen anything like it. There was so much. I was scared it was going to get on the bedspread, fearful that I would be questioned by my mother and I wouldn't know what lie to tell. I wondered if I was able to do the same thing. Needless to say, I was so fascinated after that day that Craig and I got together quite often to explore the far

reaches of space and boldly go where at least I, had never gone before. Our explorations took us under the school's bleachers, to the gym locker room, and even to restaurant bathrooms. We couldn't get enough of each other. No, we weren't able to show off our revolution in the school hallways like other kids did but it was happening at last and I was very cool with that.

Inevitably Craig called me at home one day. I could tell by the tone of his voice that something was wrong.
"What's going on?" I asked.
"Oh,"... my throat got a lump in it and I started to tear up.
"When?" I asked.
"My Dad is already gone will be moving sometime next week". Craig said over the phone.
I tried to lighten the mood.
"So you want to come over this weekend and hang out?"
"Yeah, that'd be cool if I'm not stuck here with my mom packing," Craig said.
That is just what happened. Craig and I never got to hang out again before he left.

Finding excuses for being out of class to hook up with Craig made life exciting. I now had lost two friends due to Daddies having to go to work.

CHAPTER 3

My disdain for school at its tasks continued to grow. I think Dad
thought I was just lazy. I think Mom thought I had a learning disorder.
The psychologist identified me as a strong-willed child, whatever that
means. I kind of liked that term though. To me, it simply meant I
wasn't going to do anything I didn't want to do, which basically was
true. However to hear someone outside of my family making an
assessment of me that didn't make me feel even more like crap than I
already did pretty much gave me permission to do so. I certainly was
not participating in my education at the level I knew I could. I didn't
listen. I did absorb the information. I did learn. I just never chose to
take the opportunity to demonstrate my knowledge to anyone, least of
all anyone who was in authority.

Mom was attending church at Weighton Tabernacle regularly now.
Her life was changing now that she had become a born-again
Christian through the influences of her brother, my uncle Alphie. She
would return from church bubbling over with all the new things she
had learned about God. I don't remember exactly what order it all
occurred, but eventually, my entire family had accepted Christ as our
personal Lord and Savior with Dad being the last one through the
gate. I remember praying the sinner's prayer led by my uncle Alphie
as well one day as we sat in the basement of our house. I was eleven
or so I think at the time. Even though I had confessed with my mouth
the belief In my heart part was something that was going to have to be
worked out over time. I didn't sense any kind of new special
connection with God by saying that prayer. My expectation was that

my life was going to miraculously improve now that I was saved and God wasn't mad at me anymore. Well, It didn't. I ended up failing seventh grade. I don't even remember telling my parents or how they found out or, if they found out. All I know is that the next year I had been enrolled and Weighton Tabernacle School. Weighton Tabernacle School was the Christian school that was operated by the church Mom started attending. It was a new and strange academic environment but I was grateful as I don't think I would have been able to bear repeating a grade at the same school.

Boys came to school in slacks, shirts, and ties. Girls came in A-frame skirts and coverall blouses or sweaters similar to what you might see on an episode of Leave It to Beaver. Everyone worked at their own "pace" in their paces. Paces, were the educational work booklets that students read and worked out of in the Ace Program which stood for Accelerated Christian Education. We all worked along in a quiet atmosphere, in our private cubicles as cartoon images of Ace Virtuouson, a well-groomed proper Christian white boy appeared on the pages of the workbooks giving task instructions and encouragement to complete our school work and live a good Christian life. However, Ace Virtuouson did not motivate me to want to do my school work. I was more insulted by him, but, this is what I got for failing seventh grade I guess. I would just have to make the best of it. It wasn't too difficult interacting with other kids. You really didn't have a choice. The school was so small, there wasn't really anywhere to hide. Many of the kids I already knew from church. I did meet my next long term best friend there though. Vaughn was actually one of the cool kids. Both of his older brothers also attended the school so you would be pretty stupid to pick on Vaughn. They were all kind of country looking white boys, but the girls at the school thought Chuck the middle brother, had the best looks. I thought Chuck and Vaughn were equally good-looking and friendly but Vaughn was closer to my age so, I gravitated to him for friendship. Vaughn played the drums too. We started spending a lot of time together in the church sanctuary, me on the piano and him on the drums just jammin and we were good.

Vaughn and I became very attached. We had said it to each other on many occasions that we were each other's number one. We were graced with the opportunity to build a friendship over several years. Ups and downs, birthday parties, even getting in trouble together. Vaughn also helped me overcome some of my hang-ups about the great outdoors. We rode ATVs, built fires and shot BB guns. Vaughn was the first person to try to teach me how to drive too. We used to have contests to see who could keep the cleanest bedroom and every time we'd visit each other we would hold each other accountable. Needless to say, my mother liked the fact that we were friends in this aspect. Vaughn also seemed to have a pretty good strong relationship with God, his conversations with me centered around God quite a bit. That isn't to say that we didn't get into our share of mischief. We had a lot of fun together and we were nearly Inseparable at school, youth group, choir practices, and out-of-town youth retreats. We had about 3 or 4 years of solid friendship that I often drew parallels to how Jonathan and David's relationship was in the Bible. I loved him dearly. My feelings for him were affectionate. We often told each other we loved each other and meant it. There wasn't anything I wouldn't do for Vaughn. He was my best friend.

Weighton Tabernacle, the church where my mother and later my father came into agreement to select for us all to go to and hear the word of God and grow and flourish in the things of God was in transition. Pastor Jim Mason's wife had passed away and he had now remarried. He was not a young man himself and he too passed away some months after his second marriage. The second Mrs. Mason held leadership in the church for a short time, but it became apparent that being a Pastor was not what she wanted to do at the end of her years. The search for a Pastor for Weighton Tabernacle was on. Several guest ministers came through the church to speak. Of course, kids were never really privy to knowing any of the goings-on of the selection process. But I remember when the stout German Reverend Howard J. Scheidler and his wife Ermaline were presented to the congregation as new Pastors of Weighton Tabernacle. People seemed excited and eager to have new leadership, even Mom "That Pastor Scheidler really means business around this place!", I heard her say in the car one Sunday on the way home from service. This, however, was a mixed message for me at the time as I recalled her saying something a little different to me sometime earlier in my life,

"Don't ever trust a fat preacher." was what I recall.

Pastor Scheidler preached week after week in his new role. I remember him preaching his fervent salvation messages, his reddened face, his pounding on the tall encompassing podium. I remember after some time, some said that his sermons were one-dimensional and empty but I wouldn't have known the difference. It was all Sunday morning preaching to me. I think that he may have gotten wind of some of the murmuring and questioning because I remember him making a fiery close to one of his sermons on one Sunday. He was hollering out and weeping as preachers at that time often did. He said,
 "God has been speaking to me while I've been away in retreat to get the mind of God, and God has given me a very peculiar challenge." He removed his hankie from his coat pocket to wipe his sweating brow and held it to his face as he bowed in reverence and continue to weep even harder now. "While I was on the mountain top, God spoke to me

and told me that he was going to anoint me... Jesus, I want your anointing! He wept. He spoke to me and told me that I would receive a double portion anointing and that as the weight comes off, the anointing will come on!"

The crowd roared, clapped and praised God.

In the weeks to come though, I noticed that the big messy guy who always sat in the back of the church and never really said anything to anyone, the biggest guy in the church, he was even bigger than Pastor Scheidler, He was suddenly Pastor Scheidler's right-hand man. Standing them next to each other, Scheidler looked small. The big guy got a full makeover and went from wearing jeans and a messed up t-shirt and having mussed up hair, to wearing a suit, suspenders, and grooming that even the host of Queer Eye For The Straight Guy might admire. This all happened in the space of about a week. He would always be seen next to Scheidler after services. It was as if Scheidler was trying to create some kind of optical illusion that he was losing weight. I suppressed the doubt I was having about his character. It wasn't right to question the man of God, was it? You don't fool me one bit though. I know crafty when I see it.

We were at church every time the doors were open, plus I attended school there. When I participated in sports there were days when I would arrive for school at 7:30 a.m. and would be on the church grounds until service was over for that night around 9:30 pm. My life was inundated with church. Jim and Tammy Faye Baker, Pat Robertson, Oral Roberts, Jerry Falwell, Jimmy Swaggart, Billy Graham, Chuck Swindoll, Kenneth Copeland, Fred Price, James Roberson, and Marilyn Hickey were all in between. I remember when a young CC Winans was cutting her teeth in the gospel circuit on the PTL show with Jim and Tammy Faye Baker.

These were just some of the hallmark teachers of the day in the Evangelical Christian movement. All of them were word of faith teachers. They taught a doctrine that said all things were possible. Miraculous healing, financial success, marital restoration, freedom from whatever sinful bondage you could ever have or imagine. Prayer, fasting and believing in Jesus and his power through the Holy Spirit was the answer to all of it. Believers had free and unlimited access to all of these blessings.

It was reinforced in us that as believers we could live victorious lives free from the bondage of our sins. However, if you were a person who for whatever reason were not or unable to live that kind of victorious life you must be doing it, or something wrong. If you were at the prayer altar too many times for the same thing then you might have a demon in you. If you had a demon in you, you might not really be saved because God's spirit could not possibly occupy the same space as a demonic spirit. So they had to cast the demon out first and then you had to get saved, be baptized in water, and then get baptized in the Holy Ghost with the evidence of speaking in tongues and then, you might can live victoriously for Christ.

Of course homosexuality, abortion, and premarital sex were the big no-nos, so being a Christian in this particular bubble was pretty much synonymous with being a Republican.

Strangely enough though, aside from always having to stay under the radar to hide my sexuality, I liked church, but I still used to get angry when I didn't have the option to take a break from it all. During much of my time in school, I would daydream a lot just so I could have some thoughts of my own sometimes, it's what got me into a lot of trouble. I would receive demerits for constantly having to be redirected to focus on my schoolwork. I eventually got tired of hearing them call my name and interrupting my personal thoughts, so I decided I would look studious by writing my thoughts down. It was a brilliant solution. I could be inside my own head all day long and not be bothered as I appeared to be doing school work. Everything was great until I decided to share my thoughts with someone. Trey Walker was the newest kid in school. We'd known each other for a week or two. He was a flashy, slick tongue black boy that all the girls, black and white we're falling out over. I'd be lying if I said that wasn't the case for me too. I decided to share my inner thoughts with Trey. I had used my many schoolwork hours and notebook paper writing a steamy erotic story. After some conversations I had had with Trey already, I had a feeling he would probably appreciate it. Trey never got the chance to read it though. Mrs. Mulldini, the Learning Center monitor, swooped in from around the corner and intercepted my writings as I was passing them to Trey in the cubicle behind me. My heart immediately sank into my stomach. Oh my God, how could this happen, I thought. Mrs. Mulldini set the pages on the teacher's desk just laying there and plain view. I went to Mrs. Mulldini privately and pleaded with her to please return my papers to me as they were very private and despite how it looked, they were not just notes being passed. Although I could tell she was wavering she chose to remain firm and would not return them. The pages were passed on to Mr. Gunther the Teacher and then to Mr. Chancer the Principal and then on to Pastor Scheidler. I guess they felt my writing was so offensive it needed to go all the way to the top. I was mortified. This wasn't the first time however issues had arisen with what was termed as my "preoccupation with sex" at school. I had initiated some personal sessions with Pastor Scheidler to seek guidance to help me get things under control. I felt guilty about how my behaviors were impacting my family, most of all my mother. Pastor Scheidler would listen intently to the things I would tell him and offer suggestions to help me keep my mind off sex.

He told me that whenever I was having thoughts of a sexual nature and felt I was unable to control them that he had already worked it out with Principal Chancer that I should come to his office and talk. This time when I entered Pastor Scheidler's office he was still holding the pages I had written. His face was flushed. As I sat down in one of the soft chairs he asked me,

"What made you write this down? I could see steam rising from it when they brought it in here."

I just shrugged my shoulders. "My thoughts were just running and I thought it would help to write them down," I said.

"This is really hot." he said raising his eyebrows."What do you think should happen? he asked.
"What do you mean?" I asked. "I was just writing my thoughts down. It wasn't anybody's business but mine."
"But you were going to let another kid read it." Pastor Scheidler said.
"My business as well!" I retorted.
"Well, we're going to have to come up with something. I can't just let you slide without doing anything. I'll have the whole education staff all over Me."
It was becoming clear to me that Pastor Scheidler didn't really have an interest in punishing me.

"Let me think about it for a while, you can go back to class now." He told me.

Our Gymnasium had a balcony over it that served as the cafeteria. We were all eating lunch when I saw him come through the far gym door. He motioned to me with his hands for me to come with him.

"Ooooh! You're in so much trouble, The Pastor wants to meet with you! You are so dead!" Some of the kids heckled as I dragged the remainder of my lunch from the table and made my way downstairs and across the length of the gym toward Pastor Scheidler standing on the other end. We walked over to the Pastor's office. When we got there he said he wanted me to help him carry some boxes over to the parsonage. I was really glad that he didn't seem mad at me given everything that had just happened. I grabbed the boxes and we made our way over to the parsonage which was on the church property as well and where Pastor Scheidler and his wife were living. When we stepped inside he had me take the boxes to the garage. I remember there was an old antique chest of drawers there in the garage. I remember him going in the top drawer and taking something out just as I set the boxes down on the ground where he told me.

When we went back inside he asked me if I had been able to finish my lunch. I said no and he offered me something to eat. I think he'd let me make a bologna sandwich and drink some pop. I sat down in his recliner chair to eat my sandwich and he asked me about my story and how did I come up with such vivid descriptions. I just shrugged my shoulders and kept munching away.
"That story was more descriptive than anything I've ever read like it, Ferron. Have you ever seen people having sex before?" He asked.
"Not really, no," I said.
"I mean it seems to me that the only way you would be able to be so descriptive in your story is if you had seen it before. I just wondered. Would you like to see what it's really like?" walking toward the television set and removing the object from his pocket that he had previously taken from the drawer in the garage. He pushed the VHS cassette into the VCR and the images hit me in the face like cold clay. My eyes were glued. Strangely enough, though I wasn't shocked at what was happening. Somehow it felt completely natural. Inside I was

okay with it. Or maybe I just felt like I had a new secret. I was feeling content with the fact that all of these punitive responses I was getting from authority figures regarding my adolescent sexual acting out, may very well have been overreactions. I mean, here was the Pastor of our church enjoying sex just like I do and he was in authority over all those who had previously shaken their fingers at me. It was the first time I felt without condemnation. He was a cool Pastor. I just kept watching. He kept watching me. I tried to be cool, to keep acting natural like it was nothing new to me. But I was getting excited from the video and it showed.

Suddenly the phone rang and Scheidler sprang toward the TV set, answering the phone and turning the TV off simultaneously. He leaped so fast that it startled me and I slightly jumped from my seat as well.

"Okay... tell him I'll be back in my office shortly... bye." He said.

He hung up the phone and he said, "We have to get going, I have a meeting and they are going to be looking for you back in school."

"Okay," I said.

"Wait a minute! You can't go back like that, is that thing going to go down?"

"It will by the time I get back," I said.

"You sure?"

"It'll be fine." I cinched my pants up and adjusted myself so my evidence would not be noticeable. I walked out of the small house and headed back to school. When I got back to school everyone was back at their individual cubicles studiously working. Arnie Lutz, resident school genius and nosey ass who sat next to me asked me grinning, "What happened? I saw you leave with the Pastor."

"It was nothing. He just wanted to talk to me."

"Did you get in trouble?"

"No Arnie, he just wanted to talk to me and it was kind of private, okay?"

"Alright," Arnie muttered.

Days at school were never the same. Counseling sessions with Pastor Scheidler had become more frequent, like two or three times a week. The content of my visits were becoming more involved. Jacking off, him giving me blow jobs, him wanting me to fuck him all became common. The visits moved from the parsonage to the room on the back side of Weighton Tabernacle's Sanctuary platform and most frequently Scheidler's office right before Sunday services. I remember coming away from visits with his scent on me. It was a mixture of Ralph Lauren Polo Cologne and the smell of onions that would emanate from his pores. Onions because he would eat onions like they were fucking apples.

CHAPTER 4

The school years continued to go by, filled with many incidents indicating my rebellion against the idea of God and virtually every authority figure I encountered. Just because I stopped giving a fuck, I left pornographic images in Mr. Chancers desk drawer and sexually acted out with classmates, there was truancy, vandalism, theft, sneaking out of the house at night, experimenting with alcohol. All while still going to church, youth group, and spiritual youth retreats, singing in the choir and attending Sunday school. After all, who on earth did I need to listen to anymore, now that I was in with the Pastor? The only one I had to answer to was God and God didn't seem to have any problem with what was happening. He wasn't intervening. He wasn't stopping it. There was even a time when Pastor Scheidler arranged for me to have sex with an out-of-town woman at the parsonage for which I was paid $160. Who knows how much he made. Mom and Dad were oblivious to the goings-on. I think they must have thought I had just lost my mind.

They kept on trying to get me to be on track with my walk with God and teach me right from wrong. But my miseducation process was already much further along than they could have ever known. I was maturing physically through my teen years, filling out in places becoming better looking even to myself.

Vaughn and I had reached a pinnacle in our friendship. We were even more inseparable than ever. He confided in me quite a bit after he had started a little controversy of his own in the church. Vaughn started dating Karla a girl who attended Weighton Tabernacle. She was fun to be around most of the time until things didn't go her way. Then we would all have to experience the moodiness, the waterworks and the frequent trips to the ladies room so she could pull herself together.

The biggest issue that faced Vaughn and Karla dating in the church was that Vaughn was white and Karla was black. Their relationship threw both of their families into private turmoil. Both sides tried to explain to their children in politically correct Christian-ese language that there are so many issues to face just being a couple or a married couple without throwing in the complications of race issues. They knew full well they didn't want that girl marrying a white man and definitely the same was true vice versa. Their boy was not going to marry no black girl. No matter how any of our families tried to sugarcoat it and remain" brothers and sisters" in the Lord, that was the real issue. None of it mattered to me though, until Vaughn started spending more time with Karla than he did with me.

I couldn't see it then but in hindsight, it appears that Vaughn and Karla were just determined to prove everybody wrong about their relationship. The opposition just drove them more into each other's arms. I became very jealous of their relationship and I made no secret of my growing disdain for Karla.

Once, Karla brought me one of her school photos. She had signed the back of it with something friendly and the last two digits of the year. I held onto the picture throughout service. Vaughn and Karla were sitting together during service that day. Vaughn used to sit with me and my family during service. I found myself becoming overcome with rage and tears as I sat there. Before I knew it I had crumbled up Karla's picture into a ball in my fist. I walked out of service much in the way she often did when things didn't go her way. I made my way to the men's room to regain my composure. On my way back to the service I passed the coat room, found Karla's coat and pushed the balled up picture into her coat pocket. I hoped she would find it and come and confront me so that I could go off on her. It never happened though.

Going to youth group was always a lot of fun for me though. I couldn't wait for Friday nights when we met in the chapel. The chapel was a smaller sanctuary in another part of the church where we conducted our own services and also where we had chapel services for school. Youth services were a lot more high-energy than the adult services. It was always fun to connect with all the kids in the church, to socialize and catch up on the what's what and who's who. Our youth Pastor was Alfonso Delgado at the time. He was a heavyset Puerto Rican man we affectionately called Al. He was a freshly-minted graduate of God's Mountain Bible University in Barrington Rhode Island. We all thought he was really cool. He really had what it took to move the Youth Department forward and kept us all excited about God and loving each other. He never talked down to us or used condemnation to try to get through to us. I often confided in Al when I was going through stuff. He was always great to talk to. His sense of humor always made things seem like they weren't as bad as I had perceived them to be. He taught me how to laugh and have joy in spite of adversity. Al, started a Youth Choir in which many of us participated.

We practiced on Wednesday nights with Pete, Leila, and Miesha as musicians and directors.

Leila and Miesha were Karla's older sisters. The three of them often sang together as the Lawson sisters. Vaughn, Karla and I were long-term members of the choir. Vaughn played the drums, Karla sang alto and I was a tenor. It was exciting for me because it was a facet of music I had not explored. I was learning about things I actually had interest in, in a fun environment.

It was a brisk December Saturday. It was Vaughn's birthday and he and I planned a big party and invited the youth leaders and everybody from the youth group out to his house. You could tell Vaughn's mom had put in a lot of time getting their house together. There were decorations everywhere in the house and the basement had been arranged and decked out to accommodate guests. I knew this was a task because I remember the way the basement looked beforehand from my many prior visits to the house.

There were streamers and glitter and happy birthday signs. Vaughn had connected the basement lights to a dimmer switch and brought the lights down low. Then we put on some music, and soon the atmosphere became much like a nightclub. Many of us were feeling the urge to dance but we were holding back because of our strict Christian upbringings. Finally, Anette Granger, one of the youth leaders who also directed the praise dance teams of the church, broke the ice and started to move to the music. Soon everybody was dancing and having a good time. Even Al, who showed up later acting crazy like he often would, came down the stairs boppin' from side to side and snapping his fingers to the beat of the music, and yelled out to everybody,

"I know y'all ain't dancing to worldly music down here!" And then fell out laughing.

The party was a great success we all had a great time. However, Jenna Willard, Vaughn's scorned ex-girlfriend, was in rare, no actually, common form. Bitterness about Vaughn breaking up with her had gotten the best of her. When the party was over, Jenna went to her Mother distraught. She reported that the Youth Department and leaders were all in a backslidden state, Meaning that since we were all dancing to music that was not sacred in nature, we had all sinned and fallen short of the glory of God. Of course, since the apple never falls far from the tree, Jenna's mother was in the Pastor's office at her very next opportunity. She informed him of the ills that took place at Vaughn's birthday party amongst the youth group, the choir members, as well as the leaders.

Next thing we knew there was a fiery sermon being preached about sanctification and living separate holy lives unto God. The choir was suspended from ministry for a time. I also remember being confronted by my mom about the incident. At this time she had more deeply bought into the church's teachings.

"What happened at the party?" She asked.
"We were just having a good time mom," I replied.
"Was there dancing going on?"
"Yeah?"
"Were you dancing?"
"Yeah?" Her lips tightened in dismay has she made that face that mothers make to make you feel even more guilty than God ever would without even saying a word. I really did not understand what the big deal was. Other parents had to deal with their kids being out in the

street shooting up dope, killing and being killed and we were falling out about dancing. I didn't get it.

Al was becoming a more desirable parent figure for many of us due to his non-judgmental approaches. He expressed to me privately once how he thought the actions of some church members in regard to Vaughn's party were absurd. I agreed. So a few days later I went to see Pastor Scheidler. However, I didn't have that usual look of curious innocence on my face.

"Hey, Ferron how are you?"

"Fine."

"You okay?"

"Nope", I said popping my lips on the letter p.

"What's wrong?"

"How is it that you can sit down the whole youth choir for dancing at a party, but you can still go on preaching every Sunday knowing what we do together?"

Scheidler glared at me and turned so red he looked as if his top we're going to blow up. But in a calculated response that resembled that of the Grinch from the popular Dr. Seuss cartoon. You know that part when the Grinch's whole countenance changed when he thought of the perfect lie to tell the little who girl when she questions him why he's taking their Christmas tree up the chimney.

Ferron, everyone doesn't always understand things the way you and I do he said. Sometimes we have to respond immediately to what's in front of us because that is the only thing we can see right now. You understand what I'm saying, right?

Yes, but it isn't fair that the youth choir has to be sat down for doing nothing wrong. Not even everybody who is in the youth choir was at that party. This is all because Jenna is mad that Vaughn won't go out with her anymore, and you being afraid of her mother.

Well Ferron, I still have obligations to uphold here.

Well, there has to be another way, you do understand what I'm saying, right?

The following Friday night in the youth group there was a meeting with Pastor Scheidler. He informed us that due to a lack of all the information being clearly presented, his decisions regarding youth choir were premature, and the suspension was being lifted. There was applause and appreciation. Overall the group was pleased with the decision, but many were bewildered by his change of heart and wondered what caused it. I had never felt more empowered in my entire life up to this point. But I kept my mouth shut.

CHAPTER 5

Al often planned outings and trips for us to go on. We had winter and summer weekend retreats. We even got to go out of town. Canton, Williamsport, Hershey Pennsylvania, Washington DC, the Grand Hotel at PTL in North Carolina, Fishnet rallies in Virginia. We always had a ball. When there were events we had to sing for we would practice our harmonies on the way and sing on the bus the whole trip wherever we were going. I remember once having to do a solo for the choir, but I lost my voice from singing so much before arriving there.

Canton Pennsylvania sticks out to me. We were going there to sing at a church for their weekend explosion or something. Some of the church members in Canton had opened their homes to allow us to stay for the weekend. Vaughn and I told Al that we wanted to be able to stay in the same home together. He was able to make that happen. We ended up staying in a very nice country home that was set on a dairy farm. We arrived on Friday night very late. I think that we had missed the commencement service because we got lost on the way.

We were introduced to the family and shown to our room for the night. They had made very nice accommodations for us. They had two boys of their own from what I remember. Their older son was away at school or the military and the other was slightly younger than Vaughn and I. They gave us the older boys Loft bedroom but we had to share the bed. That wasn't a problem because Vaughn and I were still the best of friends. We practically shared everything.

We were like brothers. We all woke that morning to the smell of bacon frying and I wondered to myself if Paw had got up early and slew a pig just for us. Vaughn and I had done our routines and got ourselves neatly pressed and dressed like proper city boys should and went downstairs for breakfast. The young boy of the family came bounding down the stairs in nothing but his underwear, complaining to his mother that he could not find anything to wear. "
Go look in the basement in the laundry boy." she playfully scolded. The boy had caught my attention, not only for his nearly nude appearance, but the carefreeness of the relationship between him and his mother struck me. I thought it was nice. I would have caught hell for running around the house shirtless let alone pantsless.

We ate a delicious breakfast with the family. We were told that we could hang out around the property but to be ready around 12 for the tour. Apparently, the dairy farm where we were staying was one of the highlights of the town, and the visit here by the youth explosion participants was on the itinerary for the weekend. "Great." I thought. We are going to get to meet every cow in the barn up close and personal. I just knew I did not come on this trip to be out here milking cows!
But actually, the tour turned out to be quite interesting, educational and hilariously memorable. There was a girl there from another city who apparently had not intended on touring a dairy farm either, only

she was quite a bit more vocal about it. She stepped off the van fussing, dressed head-to-toe in a summer white two-piece pantsuit and matching patent leather white flats. Her brunette hair was teased out to its prettiest fullest length and she clutched at a plastic white purse that she probably had nothing in. She just knew she was too cute for any of us or anything this dairy farm had to offer. She huffed and rolled her eyes all the way through the tour. We walked through the area where all the cows had been stalled and Mr. Dairy Farmer was explaining to us how the milking machines worked. Meanwhile, Miss Congeniality had just about had it when the cow to the left of her, feeling nature's call, raised its tail, and sprayed little missy and her summer whites down with a good 5 to 10 pounds of cow patty. Her shrills and other kids laughter fill the air. All 10 of her fingers pointed straight up in the air as her bugged eyes darted around the room like Sissy Spacek's did in that movie Carrie. Some tried to help her but there was nothing that could be done. Her group's chaperone had to take on the role of fashion paramedic and whisk her off as this crisis had escalated to alert orange status. It took some time to get the rest of us under control and I think even Mr. Dairy Farmer had difficulty remaining mature.

Later that day we went to the church where the youth services were being held. Our Choir sang in its typical glorious fashion and we were preached a fiery evangelistic style message by the preacher of the evening. There was an ice cream social at the church's annex across the street following the service where we got to meet many kids who shared common Faith from around the region. Little missy Miss Congeniality was nowhere to be found, or at least I never saw her again. After the ice cream and some fun and games, it was getting late so we headed back to our various host homes to get some shut-eye. Vaughn and I were brought back to the dairy farm and went to our room. We stayed up talking for a while recapping the day's events. We were trying ever so hard to keep our laughter to a dull roar as not to disrupt our host's household. We talked about our friendship, we talked about our futures, we talked about Karla. Vaughn tried to assure me that his relationship with Karla wasn't taking away from his friendship with me. I told him that when the three of us were together I often felt like the third wheel and that he seemed to prefer spending time with her more than he did with me. We would talk on the phone and he would say he needed to get off to keep the line free because she was going to be calling him. Yes, this was, of course, a time before call waiting or maybe neither one of our Dads wanted to pay the extra charge for it to be added to the phone line. Vaughn hugged me and told me he loved me. It was in the same way we often had done and said to one another in the past. We talked all night it seemed until we drifted off to sleep, or until he did, or so I thought. I was wide awake and feeling very close to Vaughn. I placed my arm across him ever so gently so I wouldn't wake him. He didn't seem to be disturbed so I moved in closer to him and just held him. Vaughn took a deep breath and rolled onto his side with his back to me but he was even closer to me now than before. I just put my arm across his torso. He backed up into me closer. I loved Vaughn so much it made my chest hurt. I wanted to hold him close to me and I didn't want to let him go. I had this time to be with him without Karla interrupting. I didn't want there to be any barriers between us. I put my hands across his chest. I unfastened his pajama top ever so gently in what seemed to take like an hour. Vaughn rolled over again this time toward me in a motion that practically Freed him completely from his pajama top. I touched his stomach as we laid there face-to-face, my eyes open, and his closed. I lowered my hand gently into and between his pajama bottoms and his underwear. Vaughn rolled over again away from me. My hand still inside worked as a lever moving Vaughn's bottoms down around his hip and then his thigh as he moved. I put my hand inside his underwear. As our semi-slumbered choreography progressed

Vaughn's shirt came completely off. His bottoms were around his ankles and his legs spread open looking very inviting. I, of course, accepted the invitation. Before I knew it, I dove under the covers with my head visiting places on Vaughn I hadn't imagined going. Vaughn was growing inside my mouth and he was starting to breathe heavily. I could feel his balls tense up and that signature pulsation of his shaft and his wet warmth filling my mouth. When he came Vaughn started to laugh. My heart was leaping with joy.

"What's so funny?" I asked giggling with him. He was silent. Vaughn got out of the bed and went to the bathroom.

"What's wrong?" I implored.

"What were you doing?" Vaughn asked

"What?' I said.

"You were sucking my…"

"Don't you mean what were we doing? Vaughn, I know you're not trying to say you were asleep all this time and that I got you out of all your clothes and made you cum and you had no clue what was happening. Come on Vaughn be for real."

"It shouldn't have happened", Vaughn said.

I tried to hug him and he pushed me away.

"Vaughn, Oh my God I-I'm sorry. I said as I started to cry. You laughed because you thought you were getting back at me? You cumming in my mouth was about retaliation? You thought I'd be pissed off. SHIT, Vaughn, if that's how you felt about it why didn't you stop me sooner?!"

He was silent.

"Vaughn, please talk to me."

He was silent

"Dammit!," I tearfully whispered.

I went and got back into bed and hid my face in the pillows. Vaughn came and got back into bed but slept with his head at the foot of the bed. There were only a few hours left before the sun was going to come up and the smell of bacon would again fill the air of that Canton Pennsylvania country house.

"You guys were up pretty late you awake? Said Ma dairy farm as she sat at the breakfast table. My eyes felt puffy from crying and lack of sleep.
Yeah, I just wasn't feeling so well last night, I'm okay though. I said.

We rode to church that morning and gathered for Sunday service. Vaughn still hadn't spoken a word to me. There was a Sunday picnic in the park after service with games and more fun for all, except me. Vaughn spent the entire afternoon with Karla. She noticed by his demeanor that something was wrong with him. Later Karla walked past me and glanced at me with an unpleasant knowing look. I pulled Vaughn aside and asked him,
"What did you tell her? I know you told her something!"
"Look, I didn't tell her anything. She just knows that I'm upset and that it has to do with you, okay?"
He went back over to Karla and they walked away somewhere. I just sat there at the picnic bench by myself for a long time. I remember somebody walking by and saying,
"What's wrong with you honey, you look like you just lost your best friend."
I waited until they got far enough away until my eyes felt as though they would burst from their sockets for the well of tears behind them.

CHAPTER 6

Some weeks had passed after we got back home. Vaughn and I were still estranged. I tried calling to talk to him but our conversations had nowhere near the depth they once had. Apparently, the questions that were brought to the surface by our interactions were burning so very intensely inside that, Vaughn had to talk to someone. I was walking in to see Scheidler in his office and passed Vaughn on his way out.

"Hey Vaughn," I said sheepishly. He kept walking and didn't respond. I was giving him the benefit of the doubt because I had spoken to him so softly that maybe he didn't hear me.

As I walked in, Pastor Scheidler was looking at me with an inquisitive glance.
"What?" I asked.
"Did something happen between you two?" He asked.
"What do you mean?" I asked, not really realizing at the time how unethical this man was by immediately disclosing to me the content of a private counseling session of the person who just left the room.

"He says he has concerns about his friendship with you because he thinks you're gay, Scheidler said.

"What!!??!"

"Calm down," Scheidler said.

I proceeded to tell him exactly what happened that night in Canton. He listened intently and seemed to be turned on at the same time. I can't say how it happened exactly, whether Vaughn was talking to others or if Scheidler again just couldn't help himself, but the story broke and spread across the church like wildfire. Everyone seemed to have bits and pieces of the truth, but the core was still there that Vaughn and I had some kind of sexual encounter together. We were sat down from all participation in ministry and even Scheidler could not reverse it this time without calling his own stance on Christian righteousness into question. I remember Vaughn making his way up to play the drums one Sunday and being turned away at the platform doors. I was no longer allowed to play the piano or sing in the choir. Scheidler, however, he continued to make his fat ass across the platform to the podium to preach every Sunday. I was infuriated by all the double standards. My name was being splattered all over the church and I was having to endure the ravings of embarrassed parents at home. Vaughn at least had the benefit that his parents no longer attended Weighton Tabernacle anymore, but he still had his own private hell to endure I'm sure. He pulled me aside outside service, angry.

"What the fuck is going on?" How is all this getting around the church? Vaughn exclaimed.

"Vaughn, I have been trying to talk to you. I just wish you would have talked to me."

"So you went and told everybody what happened to get back at me for not talking to you?'

"No Vaughn. Look, I know things haven't been right between us since Canton, but I would not do that to you. You want to talk to someone I know, but I think you picked the wrong guy." I said.

"What do you mean?"

"Scheidler told me everything you told him. But you didn't tell him everything." I said.

"He told you what I said?" Vaughn asked.

"Yes, and then I told him everything Vaughn, but only because I thought you were trying to make me look bad. He must have said something to someone else too cuz I haven't said anything to anybody else and it sounds like you haven't either."

"You expect me to believe that Pastor Scheidler is a gossip?" Vaughn yelled.

"Vaughn, there's a lot of things you just don't know.

"Well enlighten me, Ferron, if we have any chance at a friendship ever again, you need to tell me."

"Y'all need to come back in service now, directed Sister Pointe. Myra Pointe was a tall black authoritative usherette who was not to be played with. Vaughn and I immediately had to break up our conversation and go back into service. Vaughn's last statement was ringing in my head. I had told no one of the things that had transpired between Scheidler and me. I wanted more than anything to be friends with Vaughn again. Vaughn was sitting next to me in service and we could hear two women behind us they were holding hands and praying, binding the spirit of homosexuality. I turned around and whispered to the both of them, by virtue that you two are sitting here so close to each other and holding hands. I'm praying to God that you both are able to see your lesbian tendencies as the sin it is, as you commit it right here in God's house, and seek to overcome it. Shaken, they let go of each other's hands and ceased from their beseeching the throne. Vaughn snickered...

Vaughn came to pick me up for lunch the next Saturday for us to have a chance to hang out and talk. We made small talk at first but he made a point to remind me that he wanted me to tell him what was going on. I resisted at first but finally, I told him. He looked as if he wasn't sure what to believe. I told him that there was a lot of things that I didn't believe in anymore, but that I did believe in our friendship and I had never been dishonest with him. After that, Vaughn and I started building our friendship again. There were times when we were seen hanging out together. I didn't drive yet so sometimes Vaughn would pick me up on his motorcycle. We would take off around the city, me on the back and my arms around his waist to support myself on the bike. I think secretly neither one of us minded being that close to one another again. Rumors flew anyway. It got back to me that a youth leader made a comment after we left her house one day, "you would think after all this mess that they would stay away from each other. Now it seems like they're more in love than ever."

Vaughn was house-sitting for a family member of his one weekend. He invited me over to hang out with him one night. I told my mom I was going to his house as she would never have agreed to it if she knew there would be no adult supervision. When I got there he told me that Karla had been over to visit already so we would be able to hang out on interrupted. We watched movies, ate snacks and played video games till we tuckered out. We were both ready to lay down when Vaughn said,
"Come here, I want to show you something." He led me to the master bedroom. "I want to show you how cool this room is."
"Isn't this your Aunt and Uncle's room? Should we be in here?" I asked.
"It's okay, come on, this is where I've been sleeping anyway since I've been over here, check it out." He patted on the mattress and told me

to sit down. I didn't really notice anything special about the room and I was starting to think something was up. Vaughn had a little practical joke side to him. I remember once asking him to bring me some Kool-Aid, when he brought it back I was pleasantly surprised that he had spiked it with some vodka.

"Just stay here, I'm going to get something," Vaughn said.

When he left the room, a few seconds later the lights went out. Images started being projected on the wall in front of the bed, images much like the ones I had seen in Pastor Scheidler's parsonage. Vaughn came back in the room laughing hysterically.

Okayyy? I said. Vaughn came in and plopped himself on the bed next to me, still cracking up. "I found this the other night he said that's why I'm sleeping in here." He said laughing through his talking.

Vaughn started taking off his shirt and scooting under the covers. I just did the same. After everything we've been through I wasn't expecting him to go here with me again but it was starting to look like he wanted a repeat performance of Canton.

The video ended and I was pretty worked up by the images I had seen. Vaughn was lying next to me shirtless with his eyes closed appearing to be asleep. Less inhibited this time, I put my arms around him and held him. I slipped my hand down his pants and got him out of them, in a much shorter time than the last. I definitely was not as concerned about whether I would wake him or not. Before I knew it my head was under the covers again pleasing Vaughn to completion. This time there was no laughter or dash for the bathroom. There was no argument that ensued following. When I emerged from underneath the covers I just put my arms around him and held him next to me all night as he pretended to sleep. Then we both finally slept

Vaughn awoke apologetically. He just kept saying he was sorry.

"Sorry for what?" I said.

I told you before this shouldn't have happened, and then I set you up to do it again by playing that movie and getting you all turned on."

"What?" I asked. "Vaughn, your honesty is getting a little better but you seem to be getting something mixed up. I really wish you would stop trying to play Mr. Innocent trying to make it seem as though you don't want any of this to happen, until after it has already happened! If you don't want to have sex with me anymore just say so and trust me it will never happen again!"

We went back and forth a few times debating. We totally overlooked the fact that we were arguing in his Aunt and Uncle's bedroom naked on opposite sides of the bed. If this wasn't a lover's quarrel, I don't know what one is.

CHAPTER 7

Vaughn still was not ready to confront the inner conflicts our interactions were causing him. I, wasn't ready to go backward. Secretly, I had hoped that he would run to me instead of run away. We all have wishful thinking.

It was a warm partly cloudy Saturday in August 1984. I had invited all my friends from church that I thought would come. I had lost track of my friends from secular schools. I was turning 16 and I wanted to have the party of the century. Mom made the cake. Dad had planned to barbecue and my sister was about the house helping with the decorations. I was out in the yard setting up badminton nets, horseshoe games, and stuff for potato sack races. I really wanted this to be the event of the summer that everybody would remember and the fact that it was MY birthday would be how everyone would remember it.

This is also when I started developing the opinion that God didn't care for me very much. I started to feel like, yeah God loves me but it was only out of obligation to his own word. But I didn't think he really liked me very much. I was feverishly trying to make everything perfect for my guests with games and places to sit and music. In the midst of my labors, in spite of my prayers earlier in the week, a torrential downpour ensued. As the sprinkles began I found myself out in the front yard exercising whatever faith I believed that I had. With my hands raised to the sky like Storm the weather which from the X-Men, I bound the works of the air, wind, and sky that had been sent to destroy my party. As the rain increased my cries turn to "GOD PLEASE NO!" My hands felt to my sides along with the rain from the sky and I walked defeated, soaked and tearful into the house. The cloud from this particular rainstorm would follow over the top of my head for a long time.

Most of my guests arrived late. I laid in my bed for a long time wondering if anyone was coming at all. Vaughn said he was going to come but he couldn't come till late because he had to work. Although I wanted him to be there with me the whole day, I was still looking forward to his arrival. He said that he would stay overnight and we could go to church together the next morning. I was looking forward to us being able to have another one of our deep meaningful conversations.

My guests did start showing up late in the afternoon. Trey came too. I couldn't have the outdoor bash that I had planned but we made the best of it and we had fun anyway. It was starting to get dark and the party had moved into the family room of our house because that is where the Atari was. Everybody was gathered around the TV talking, laughing and taking turns playing the video games we had. Trey and I had left the group and we were chillin in my room talking. I don't remember exactly how it happened. Trey and I had joked about being sexual with each other before but, before I knew it, my door was closed, the lights were out, our pants were around our ankles and we were all the way at it.

The headlights of the green Nova Vaughn drove turned into the driveway. Vaughn was very much like family to me so I often gave him family privileges even though the rest of my family may not have been aware. Vaughn took his overnight bag from the car and slung it over his shoulder making his way to the house. The front door was open so he pulled open the screen door in came in without knocking. No one from the party saw or heard him come in because of the curtain my mom hung over the kitchen entryway in the summertime to keep the cool air from the large wall unit air conditioner contained in that area of the house. Vaughn made his way down the hallway toward my room. Unassumingly pushing on the door to open it, the sound of the door and the light from the hallway pouring in startled Trey and I. We jumped up from our positions.
"Damn, don't anybody knock anymore?" Trey barked covering his eyes. Vaughn backed up from the door and angrily turned around and started down the hallway again.
SHIT! I said.
I jumped up and fix my pants as best as I could and rushed after him.
"Vaughn!" I caught up to him and grabbed his arm softly.
"Let me go!" Vaughn said pulling his arm away.
"I don't want you to go Vaughn."
Vaughn kept walking. I was getting the impression that Vaughn was not upset about what he saw us doing but more so that it wasn't between he and I.
"Vaughn!" I started to cry. I couldn't bear the thought of him not responding to me. But then I thought you know what? He's had the chance to tell me how he feels about me. Then, I thought what if he was going to tell me tonight? Then I thought, if he wants this he can come and get it!

I watched him pull out of the driveway. I was upset with myself I had traded what I wanted as the pinnacle of my day for what I knew was going to be fleeting with Trey. But there was no way in hell I was I going to let the whole evening be a bust. I went right down that hallway to my room and found Trey still there with everything still out and ready. I closed the door I turned out the lights and Trey and I commenced to making the record books.

Later Trey and I slipped back into the party without missing a beat. All were oblivious to what had transpired that night behind the blue curtain that covered the kitchen entryway.

After all my guests had said their well-wishes, goodbyes, gave their gifts and hugs, they departed. Everyone needed to get home. After all, there was church in the morning.

A short while later while I was cleaning up, the headlights of the green Nova turned into the driveway. Vaughn came to the still open door and knocked.

"Hey man what's up?" I said opening the door to let him in.
"I didn't feel like going all the way back home," Vaughn replied.
"Well, you can stay here man if you want," I said, twisting my lips to the side.
"Duhh." He said grinning at me.

Vaughn helped me finish cleaning up and we went to bed shortly thereafter. I had had a very eventful an emotional day and was visibly exhausted. Vaughn and I slept through the night and rode to church together the next day. There was no discussion about Trey and me.

CHAPTER 8

Sean Presley Wexler. He was a clean slick-haired evangelist and faith healer that had become a regular appearance at Weighton Tabernacle. I came to believe he was a close personal friend of Pastor Scheidler. Wexler often would monologue about his many feats of faith he had encountered in his life and ministry in order to raise the faith level of congregants before moving in the spirit. He was one who would call individuals out of the audience and speak prophetically over their lives. Sometimes he would lay his hands on the part of their body that he believed God had shown him was not functioning properly and he would pray for God to heal them. It often resulted in the congregant being moved to tears, rejoicing, shouting or being slain in the spirit, and so on. That means they would fall to the floor overwhelmed by the power of God supposedly. It was a state in which it is believed that the presence of God is so strong that the human body cannot withstand it.

I was not impressed, however. Wexler was in town one weekend and he had been invited to come and participate and Weighton

Tabernacle school's Friday Chapel service. Toward the end of the service, Wexler began to operate in his anointing and was calling some of the kids out of their seats to prophesy over them. The outcomes were the same for most of the kids as they mimicked what they saw their parents doing. Wexler had a stare that made you think he was looking right through you. As he passed by where I was sitting he was saying things like "Bless you Lord, yes. I hear you, I will Lord." It was mixed with his speaking in tongues. Then his eyes making that penetrating stare were directed toward me. He pointed at me and motioned for me to move from my seat and come forward. When I got to the front he shut his eyes tightly and began weeping.

"Oh God oh, this one is so special to you. Let your anointing, a double portion of Shekaniah's anointing fall on him. His voice began to bellow, may his life touch nothing but your glo-reh, your glo-reh God!" His hand went up in the air as he prayed even more fervently and as his hand came down to touch my head, my arm went up to block his and prevent him from laying hands on me. Gasps went across the room. Wexler's eyes opened and we stood there for a moment looking coldly into one another's eyes. Wexler leaned forward and whispered to me.

"What's the matter boy, don't you want God's blessing on your life?" He asked.

I nodded my head yes. Inside I was thinking "first of all I'm not your boy and secondly my life seems to go to hell every time one of these people prays for me. If one more person lays hands on me and something bad happens I'm going to snap! If God wants me to be blessed and anointed and all, then he will see to it that it happens, hands laid on me or not.

I didn't know why God made me the way I am or why I was experiencing all the things that were happening to me. All I ever kept hearing was that God has a reason for everything and that it would make sense later. In the meantime, I really just wanted to have fun. But having fun and growing up Christian always seemed to present conflict. Let alone growing up gay.

CHAPTER 9

Some people make the mistake of thinking being gay means that a guy has a desire to be a woman. I don't think I ever wanted to really be a girl. I did admire how easy girls seem to have it when it came to getting guys to notice them.

It was the end of October and Al had the entire youth group planning a huge masquerade party. It was an attempt to give us kids something fun to do in lieu of Weighton Tabernacle's avid beliefs in opposition to celebrating Halloween. However, we still managed to have one of those cheesy, blindfolded, stick your fingers in a bowl of olives and pasta and tell them it's brains and eyeballs haunted funhouse things in the gym balcony. There was supposed to be a lip sync contest at the party and everyone was feverishly and secretly preparing their act. Tramaine Hawkins was one of my favorite gospel singers. Especially after she had released the hottest gospel song ever to be recorded in my opinion, <u>Fall Down On Me!</u>

While Mom was gone to prayer meeting one Saturday I sneaked into her makeup room in her closet. Mom, being a former model and makeup artist she had a lot of makeup, hairpieces, wigs, and costume jewelry. I grabbed some pieces that I thought she didn't use very often and went scurrying off to the bathroom. After experimenting and having to wash everything off and start over three or four times and start over, I was finished. I thought to myself "yep I can do this." It was settled I would impersonate my favorite gospel artist, lip-sync the hottest song ever and not only will I shock and amaze my friends and partygoers, but baby I'm going to win this little contest, as I snapped my fingers!

Slam! Went the back door. I had lost track of time and mom was home.
Shoot! I thought. I always tried not to be in the bathroom when Mom got home from anywhere, she already had issues with my being in the bathroom for extended periods of time. I could hear her coming down the hall and the knock on the door. Seems like those closed-door scenarios I would see on TV never worked out quite the same for me because even though Mom would knock she was simultaneously opening the door whether you responded or not. So there I stood in front of the bathroom sink, wearing my glorious rendition of Tramaine Hawkins created out of my mother's hair and makeup. My mother had this how do I handle this look on her face while I imagine hundreds of scriptures mixed with countless episodes of the Donahue show raced through her head. Not to mention she must have been suppressing the urge to just commence to whooping my ass for stealing her makeup, wigs, and jewelry.

"What are you doing?" She said calmly.
"I'm practicing for the masquerade party," I replied, thinking play innocent.

"What kind of…"

"See mom, there's going to be a lip-sync contest and I'm going to do Tramaine Hawkins, you know the gospel singer."

And this is where people will now understand why I fell out uncontrollably laughing in the middle of Jordan Peele's hit movie Get Out, as my mother's response was exactly the same as Georgina's.

"Oh no no no no no no no no no dear." She said with her sing-song voice, but her voice was not matching her facial expressions." Isn't there someone else you could pick?"

"But Tremaine is my favorite."

"Honey, I'm sorry but we're going to have to find something else for you to go as for the masquerade party. Now could you take off my things and put them BACK... where you found them."

"Yes," I said grumbling.

I was afraid, very afraid. Mom left to her own devices in the creation of Halloween costumes was very frightening at times. There was the year of the robot. I am not sure if her motivation was the TV show Lost in Space but she spray-painted a couple of boxes silver and cut holes out of the arms and eyes and one triangular hole in the front with the words "feed me" written in magic marker above it to indicate where to reach in and drop candy. People didn't get it, they just laughed and kept saying "hey honey come look at the box."

There was the year she covered my face and cold cream and pressed several raisins into the cold cream and to make the ensemble complete she added one solitary honeycomb cereal piece in the middle of my forehead. I have no idea what I was. I am sure she wasn't completely to blame. Dad, as frugal as he was, I am sure there was no way he was spending any money on store-bought Halloween costumes that I would use once in a lifetime. This time, however, Mom had gathered some old bedspreads and curtains. Probably that same blue curtain she used on the kitchen doorway to keep the cool air in,

and a purple bedspread from my sister's old bedroom sets. Somehow she fashioned me and Old-Testament style robe and a sash that Charlton Heston might have worn in the Ten Commandments.
Sure enough, I was to be Moses for the masquerade party. The Ten Commandments were scrawled on tablets of cardboard for me to carry. But there was only one command that was ringing clear in all of this. Thou shalt not do drag!

Since I was a part of the party's planning committee and it was a school day as well, I decided that my plans for the party were not going to be thwarted. I was still on the program to perform in the lip-sync contest. I would stay after school that day and help with the party set up. The night of the party we decorated the gym festively with all the fall season trimmings. Pumpkins, horns of plenty and colored leaves were placed in and about. In the center of the ceiling was mounted a mirror ball like you might see an old disco clubs. Gold, Brown Auburn streamers cascaded out from the ball to various points in the room. Weighton Tabernacle was a bit of a cutting-edge church so they had lots of lighting and sound equipment that they would utilize for their many holiday dramatic productions. It was a Friday night and service was going on for the adults in the main sanctuary of the building, so Mom and Dad would be coming later.

The time came, and I slipped into the Moses costume and waited for my parents' arrival so I could actually let them and others see me in the costume before they went into church. I would let them get their laughs as I marched around saying "let my people go!" As the kids arrived, I could see that their parents were a bit more liberal. Two of my best girlfriends from school Yvonne and Michelle whom I personally thought had the best costumes that night came as Franken-whores. They looked fantastic with their hair teased out to resemble electric shock with Frankenstein makeup, leather mini-skirts, fishnet stockings, and shiny combat boots. Luckily the day before, I managed to sneak back into Mom's closet and pull Tremaine back out by her gospel roots again and had packed her neatly into my school bag underneath Moses. Later as the party progressed, I slipped into an unused bathroom downstairs in the school area. Earlier I had jimmy-rigged the door so I would be able to get back in. I was able to make the transformation from Moses to Tremaine in about 30 minutes before I was supposed to go on. I had worked some things out with the sound and lighting guy as it related to my act ahead of time so I pretty much stayed out of sight until it was time.

The lights went down low, there was a burst of smoke on the little two-foot-high stage, the rumble of thunder and flashes of light like lightning. Then the infamous intro to Tremaine's hit song Fall Down On Me, began. As the beat and the music filled the room kids started clapping their hands dancing and getting into it. I ran out on stage and started performing the song. I was working the stage and the audience. I was twisting and twirling and shaking my groove thing like a pro. I could hear kids cracking up laughing but it didn't seem like they were laughing at me, it seemed more like they were having a good time. I was too. When it was over there was hype energy in the room. There was laughing and applause. I was the last act to go on, so I knew it was getting late I knew I had to make my transformation back into Moses before service ended and Mom and Dad came to pick me up to go home. I missed the judging so, I didn't win, but I didn't care. The rush of that feeling of acceptance even if but for a moment was worth it all to me, even the consequences I might have to suffer later for disobeying my mother.

I'm met my mother at the entrance of the gym of course dressed in the Moses costume she made for me. She looked around the gym and said "It looks like a disco in here!" and shook her head disapprovingly.

"Come on Ferron we have to go it's late." Strangely enough, though, news of my performance either never reached my parents or maybe they just decided to leave it alone. Although the latter I think is unlikely. I just put my mom's things back where I found them at my next opportunity and never bothered them again.

CHAPTER 10

My behaviors eventually got me expelled from Weighton Tabernacle School. My parents made an appointment with Mr. Fabry the Principal of Christ-Light Christian Academy on the other side of town. It was a school that was privately owned and operated by First Bible Baptist Church in Gates New York. It was a good distance from where we lived. After the interview, Mr. Fabry leaned back in his office chair and said,

"You know, it's not my customary practice to enroll students in the middle of the school year but, young man, you speak very well and I think it would be a shame to have your education interrupted."
"Speak well?" I thought to myself. What, is his expectation that all black boys my age are illiterate?"
We want you to begin classes here on Monday. He said.
"Cool," I said sarcastically.

Christ-Light was a little more rigid than Weighton Tabernacle in a lot of ways but they did utilize a bit of a more traditional academic model. We at least got to change classrooms for different subjects. They were real big on the dress code. I guess their philosophy was that somehow inappropriate clothing was directly linked to teenage pregnancy or something. They had a guard at the door, Mr. Stein. Mr. Stein was the disciplinary officer of the school, making sure everyone was in the dress code before entering. This particular day I was not wearing a belt so Mr. Stein would not let me into the school. Since I lived all the way across town there was no way for me to go and get one so I just ended up wandering the streets of Gates for a time until I got fed up and stopped a police officer.

"What's the problem?" He asked.

"Well, I don't have a way home," I said

"Why aren't you in school?"

"Well, My school insists on obstructing my education today because I'm not wearing a belt."

"What school do you go to?" asked the officer.

"Why, I go to Christ-Light Christian Academy, sir," I said in my best southern belle voice.

The officer allowed me into his patrol car and took me back to School. While I waited in the office lobby, the officer, Principal Fabry, and Mr. Stein came out.

When the officer left, Mr. Stein glared at me and said, "You can go to class now." I picked up my things slowly rolling my eyes and left for class. I don't know, maybe they got fined or something.

There were a couple of kids from Weighton Tabernacle at Christ-Light so I did get to have some familiarity in that aspect. Fred and Jeff Trummel, they were brothers who attended Weighton Tabernacle at one time and mysteriously moved to another school after their sister Ramona became an unwed mother. For her punishment, she was made to stand before the entire youth group and testify as to the ills of premarital sex. I remember her standing up there weeping and preaching to us that sex was not like it is depicted in rated R movies. I also remember being unmoved by her tears.

Fred, was tall handsome and bad-boyish. His dirty blonde hair always testing the length limitations of the dress code often covered his eyes. I sometimes think he liked it long just so he could flip it back when girls came around. Girls liked him a lot. Jeff, was the younger of the two and was still kind of rascally. Nanette, was pretty intellectual, but not so much that you couldn't have a conversation with her. She still had a sense of humor. Nanette Faison who also attended Weighton Tabernacle with her sister Tamela, who was a year ahead of her, was now an upperclassman at Christ-light. She was the only other black student besides me there, so of course, we were always the target of our peers trying to make us into a couple. Neither one of us could have been further from interested in each other romantically, but we were pretty good friends.

I was still a bit of an outsider until the following year when I met Serina McCormick. Serina was a tall white girl who was Cyndi Lauper and Madonna all rolled into one. To see her try to make her own personal style fit into Christ-Light's dress code was always fascinating to me. As weird as she might have looked to some, sometimes with the back of her head shaved with big Madonna bows tied on top of her head, her big gaudy jewelry and the rubber bracelets I still thought she was cool. All the kids liked her too. I think I admired her so much because she struck me as someone who was not going to let anyone stifle who she was, regardless of the environment. Even more so, she didn't seem to mind being friends with me. We were in most of all the same classes so we hung out all the time and I came to find out that she was just as much if not more mischievous than I. We got along great.

At Christ-Light every year they would throw their prom equivalent, the Junior-Senior banquet. I say equivalent because as you may not know in most Christian circles dancing was just not allowed. The Junior class every year was responsible for planning the event and putting it on for the Senior class. This year I was responsible for the music and entertainment. The committee decided on the theme, <u>Through the Years</u>. To accompany the theme they selected a popular Kenny Rogers song of the same title to be the theme song. However, when it was submitted to The Faculty for approval I guess since there had been no record of Kenny Rogers ever reciting the sinner's prayer, his music was deemed inappropriate for the event. The planning committee had become frantic so I stepped up to the plate and offered to write a song for the Junior-Senior banquet theme and secretly dared them to question my salvation. In about a week and a half, I had a draft of the song or at least a chorus and we brought it before the faculty. I think they were expecting to listen to another recorded song because they seemed a little taken back when I sat at the piano to play and sing the song for them. They really seemed delighted by the song as up to this point, they were unaware of my musical abilities.

"Why haven't you joined the chorus or band Ferron? You are very talented."

"Well, there isn't much room for a piano in a marching band and the last I recall the chorus was all female, besides they do well enough without me."

I was being polite.

"I knew that an opportunity for my talents would come eventually though." I explained.

I had invited two friends to the banquet, one ironically was Karla. We were to do a duet of <u>Jesus never fails</u> on the program. The other was

Nate this guy I was sort of seeing at the time. The pictures from the evening indicate that Karla was my date only because Nate and I were disallowed from taking pictures together. It was a big to-do, which resulted in my becoming indignant and driving home the point that "If I'm paying for these damn pictures I will put whoever the fuck I want to put in them!"

Subsequently, I was asked not to return to Christ-Light for my Senior year.

That following year since I wasn't in school, Dad encouraged me to enroll at the local Community College. I only agreed because I was trying to do the right thing and I was grabbing at straws for something I could do to make him proud of me. I spent one year at Monroe Community College, which was pretty much a complete waste of time other than my involvement with the Monroe Community College Gospel Choir. I got to spread my wings a bit musically in the local gospel circuit and meet other musicians and singers that helped me hone my style. Mr. Alvin Parris the Third was the instructor and even Leila Lawson from Weighton Tabernacle was a part of the group also. Leila played piano and sang and sometimes taught songs to the group.

Mister Parris also gave me the opportunity to teach a song to the group. This was my first time ever doing any kind of music with anyone else outside of Weighton Tabernacle. He allowed me to teach an original song that I had written. It was entitled His Love will Never Fail. The song was not spectacular but no one had ever really given me an opportunity to showcase my own music before. I was revelling in it.

However, the young lady in the front of the soprano section was in my opinion unnecessarily giving me all kinds of attitude during rehearsal, rolling her eyes and not giving her all to singing the parts I was teaching.

On about the third occasion, I stopped playing, turned to her and said

"There really are enough Sopranos here today your presence is not really required if this is really THAT too much for you!"

Just then Mr. Parris gently put his hand on my shoulder and motioned for me to come out into the hallway.

Reluctantly, I complied as Leila slipped on to the piano and continued the rehearsal.

In the Hallway Mr. Parris said,

"Son, you're going to be doing this for a very long time, and you are going to encounter a lot of difficult people. So it's best you learn now how to manage your feelings and how to talk to people in a way that will bring out the best in them when you're conducting rehearsals," He said, ever so gently.

"Trust me, it's rarely personal, so don't take it personally," He added.

I mean, I didn't feel like I was wrong, I didn't feel like I should have been the one pulled in the hallway, but he said it so kindly. He was so respectful, and it made me feel good that someone so musically accomplished thought well enough of my abilities to speak of them in future tense. It was by far the most significant learning experience of my entire college career.

However, I couldn't keep wasting Dad's money on classes that I had no intention of applying myself to. So since I wasn't going to be in school, I had to get a job. Dad required me to start contributing to the household.

I was really excited when I found a job at Edwards department store in Pittsville Ponds Atrium. Edwards, to me, had the feel and ambiance of the big downtown department stores, but it was really close to home. I felt like I was breaking into the world of fashion and following in Mother's footsteps who was a fashion model and the makeup artist at one time. I worked as a cashier in the men's Department until the store eventually closed for business a year or so later. I was concerned that I wouldn't be able to meet the obligations that Dad set out for me, so as soon as I got word that the store was closing, I went directly across the street to Bill Gray's hamburger restaurant to apply for a job.

Luckily, I was hired as a dishwasher. Certainly not as glamorous as Edwards but I didn't have to face the shame of being unemployed. Somehow I still managed to feel guilty and personalize the circumstances of potentially not having a job, even though the store's closing had nothing to do with me.

Working at Bill Gray's wasn't so bad. I was bussing tables and washing dishes mostly and sometimes I worked the grill. I made some pretty good friends while I was working there. One night after work I heard Michelle one of my co-workers planning to go out to the Liberty on the weekend. Michelle was a 20 something Italian girl with wavy black hair who was in my opinion, aging too fast. Either that or she just wore too much makeup. But nevertheless, she was loud and funny most of the time. I liked her.

"Yeah, it's a really cool place the music is great we should all go, Ferron, you want to come?"

"Uh Where?"

"The Liberty." She said.

"What's the Liberty?" I asked.

"It's this hot gay bar Downtown." She said with a curious side-eyed grin on her face.

"A gay bar?" I asked. I had never really heard anyone say gay in public before at least not unless they were whispering.

"Yeah, it's downtown." She said.

"Uhh... Okay, I'll think about it." I said.

Michelle's brother Mike was our boss at Bill Gray's. He was the one who hired me. I thought he was cute before I thought he was gay, but connecting the dots led me to think that maybe he was how Michelle had encountered the Liberty. The truth was I really wanted to go but I needed to figure out a good story to tell my parents if they asked why I was out later than usual, and pray that one of my co-workers could bring me home after. The last time I stayed out late was for my friend Greta's prom over the summer. I even told my Mom I would probably be out all night and I still got read the riot act when I came in.

When Friday came we closed up the restaurant and Michelle asked if I still wanted to go with them to The Liberty. I had already intended on saying yes because I made sure that I brought a clean outfit to wear. I was curious. Yeah, I knew I liked guys and all, but I wasn't sure I was ready yet for the gay label. I wanted to see what gay meant. I too still had a lot of misconceptions. Going to the bar brought many of them to the surface.

When we arrived the line to get in was all the way out into the sidewalk. Back then they would still let you in the bar even if you were underage, you just couldn't drink so they'd mark your hand with a big X in magic marker so the bartenders would not serve you alcohol. I could feel the bump of the music off in the background that got louder as we got closer to the door. Everybody seemed to be having fun, even outside in line before we got in. There was a $3 cover charge that night but for some reason, I did not have to pay. They put a big X on my hand and within minutes bursting through the crowd there was Mike, my boss from Bill Gray's, in nothing but a pair of hot pants and leather boots. Mike was a short cute Italian guy who was pretty much hairy all over and was apparently a server at this establishment.

"Hiiii Feerrron what's up! I'm glad you made it out. He said putting a drink in my hand. Baby, just drink up and put it back on the tray when you're done don't worry about that X on your hand Mama's got you covered."

Coming through the crowd and the smoke from the dance floor I could see a lot of what I considered to be pseudo drag queens coming toward me. Guys that were made up like girls, but I could still tell they were guys. At the time they were frightening to me. Mainly because of my indoctrination at Weighton Tabernacle, I had it in my head that becoming gay went in stages like a disease just like AIDS. I wasn't sure how far I really wanted to go with this. I actually believed that full-time drag queens were the final stage, and I knew I did not want to go there. I had no desire to be a woman. Hey, I was 15 and ignorant.

Eventually, the alcohol began to work its magic and I started to loosen up, dance and mingle. I was in a room jam-packed with people who were like me but didn't seem to have nearly any of the conflicted emotions I was having about life. Everyone just seemed to be happy with who they were and weren't putting on any airs. Again, I was 15 and ignorant.

Nonetheless, I had found a new home. A place where I could just be who I was one night and be someone else the next if I wanted. Eventually, I became a regular staple around the Liberty. Bartenders knew me by name and I would always be seen out in front during virtually every drag show to pay homage to the local Queens. There was Jamie Blue, Aggy Dune, Ashley Nicole, Nikki Davenport, Morgan, and even... Falexis. The Not So beloved Queen of the house.

It was The mid-80s. Tears for Fears, Karyn White, Paula Abdul, Madonna, Boy George, George Michael, and Michael Jackson were ruling the airwaves. Not to mention MTV was birthing a whole new era of visual music appreciation. It was a field day for drag performers of the day in the potpourri of great material. The first time I saw a show I really thought Jamie Blue was a woman up there singing and performing. Of course, my cocktails and the fact that up until this point I had never heard a Bette Midler live album contributed to my ignorance. Jamie's look was flawless to me, as was her performance. She had not only without error lip-synced the songs, but Miss Midler's recorded monologues as well. I was captivated.

CHAPTER 11

I walked into Scheidler's office one Friday before evening service. Wexler was there in nothing but underwear and socks. Scheidler sat behind his huge desk. I wasn't shocked, nor did they seem to be either. After all, Scheidler's office had become more of a locker room scene from gay porn to me more so than a place of biblical study or where church business was conducted. It wasn't uncommon for me to encounter semi or even complete nudity in that room. However, it seemed as though there would be no encounters for me this day as it seemed Wexler had already done the do.

"Oh, Hi Ferron," Scheidler said. "What can we do for you?"
"Nothing, I just stopped by to see you before service," I said.
"Did you need to talk to me?" He said while Wexler finished dressing.
"No, really I was just stopping in," I said
"You ready for some church?" Wexler said zipping up his pants and fastening his belt.
"Sure whatever," I said. I suppose you have another one of your great messages for us again?"

The phone rang and it was for Wexler. I used that as my opportunity to slip out of the room and not continue the conversation. Unbeknown to me at that time, earlier that day the story had broken about PTL leader Jim Baker's affair with Jessica Hahn. Wexler had been named as the man that arranged the sexual encounter between Jim Baker and Jessica Hahn. His integrity in the Christian Community had come into question. That night Wexler wept before the congregation and pled for their forgiveness for his "fall from grace" as he called it. He said he knew God had forgiven him but he could not go forward without addressing it with God's people.

The prayer line that night was not as long as it was on other nights. After service, there were reporters outside of the church trying to get the scoop on the PTL scandal. They were trying to get pictures of Wexler. My Dad just hurried us to the car to go home.

On Saturday night I snuck out of my bedroom window after dark. I planned to go out to the Liberty again. I planned it perfectly so I could catch the very last bus into town. I had not yet figured out how I would get home, but I didn't care. I would cross that bridge when I got there. I needed to clear my head. Yeah well, I caught the last bus into town but it was still early by clubbing standards, people didn't even start coming out until after midnight. When I got downtown it was still a bit dead.

Around the corner from the Liberty was a little neighborhood gay watering hole called Tara's. I decided to hang out there and have a few drinks until things livened up a bit. When I walked in it was like pieces of my life were flashing in front of me all at once. There was Mike, my boss from Bill Grays sitting on one end of the bar laughing it up with friends. There was Mr. Gallows, my piano teacher from years earlier sitting alone, drinking and not looking as well as I remembered him at the other end. And they're in the middle of the bar, also alone and nearly falling off his seat, was Wexler. His face reddened from the alcohol. I did not want to stay here. It was the first time I had been out in the gay world and encountered people who did not know I was a part of it. I turned to walk out the door quietly when,

"Hiiii Feerrrron, what's up girlfrieeend, you just going to walk out of here without saying hello?" railed Mike from the corner of the bar.

I closed and rolled my eyes in my head. I turned to him.

"Hi, Mike how you doing. I said. Wexler didn't move. Mr. Gallows remained perched on his barstool looking like old Hollywood glamour.

"No it wasn't that," I said. I was just on my way to meet somebody. Oooooh, hot date huh, what's his name, what's he look like, how big is his dick, oops, did I just go where my business ends and yours begins? Well honey that's why girls like me need to know these things, cuz if there's enough business for both of us then I won't need no business of my own then will I, you know what I'm saying?" He rambled off without taking a breath, finishing with a tilt of his head to the side, a wink and pooching his lips out.

I was waiting for Wexler to finally turn to me and recognize me, for us to have some kind of awkward interaction, but he just sat there holding his glass and looking slightly upward with glazed eyes. He appeared to be off in his own world, oblivious to all that was going on around him. I wasn't going to mess up his muse. It almost looked like he was praying. The local gay bar is not customarily thought of as a suitable environment in which someone might look for God. I didn't realize or think that at that moment he very well may have been seeking God with his cocktails and all. I just thought to myself he's so drunk, he doesn't even know what's going on. I knew he was a fuckin fake anyway. I turned toward the front door of Tara's, waved goodbye to Mike, and walked out into the warm night.

The sound of passing cars and the occasional bump, bump, bump, of someone's car stereo going by was all that was to be heard. That and the effects of the warm wind in the trees. The tall street lamps lit up Liberty Pole way where of course the Liberty was located. The music had just begun to play on the dance floor and I wasn't going to let a night of freedom get away from me. The wind was blowing into my shirt a certain way and I, was feeling very sexy.

It was still early enough that no one was posted at the door to collect a cover charge, so I got in free. Free was good, so this became my new practice whenever I went out. I would get there just as soon as the door would open to save me the three to five bucks. I figured it would be a few extra drinks for me.
"Hey Ferron,": said Jessie, the beefcake bartender smiling from behind the bar.
"Hey Jess," I said
"Rum and coke?"
"You know it, with lime please," I said flirtatiously.
Only a few people were scattered about the establishment. Video screens were rolling brightly with snippets of music videos interwoven with clips of gay porn. I remember I used to get frustrated because the porn clips would always cut out and back to the music video just when the good parts were coming up.

Soon the popular club began to fill up and the energy level rose nearly through the roof. It seemed like guys couldn't wait to come out of their clothes. Shirts off, music bumpin, rump-shakin, Queens twirling, kickin and swirlin. The party was on and the cares of the world were gone. At least for a few hours anyway. It wasn't long before I made my way to the center of the dance floor with one hand on my hip, and the other with my glass raised to the sky, and I belted out the highest glass breaking note in the song I could reach at the precise moment the music of the record had a pause to rebuild its momentum back into its groove. Everyone on the dance floor exploded with enthusiasm in response to what at that very moment had become my signature, call to the party.

I had made some friends for the night by buying them some drinks. Chanel, a not yet so polished, up-and-coming drag queen was among them. She made me feel that she had taken a liking to me, although, I wasn't sure if it was about me or the liquor I was buying. Anyway, I worked into the conversation that I needed a ride home tonight. She told me that she would work it out with her friend who had the car for the night. After the club closed, Chanel made good on her promise but when we pulled up a few houses away from where I lived, she asked could I give the driver some gas money. I thought, gas money! I just bought y'all all these drinks and all I ask for is a ride home and y'all want gas money too? It was gay-life lesson number one. It was always about the gas money honey. I slipped Chanel a $5 bill, gave her a hug and they drove off. I managed to slip back into my bedroom window and into bed undetected.

I was slow waking up that Sunday morning for church. The alcohol was still working in my system, but I managed to drag myself through breakfast and into the shower and I got dressed in my Sunday Best for church. Walking from the car to the church building obviously was more of a task than I realized. Even though I stumbled over the curb of the walkway to the entrance, I thought I was maintaining my presence pretty well. Later it became apparent to me that this was not the case.
"Ferron!" Barked Manny Lawson, Karla's little brother. You must have been really sleepy this morning, we saw you walking in and you was walking sideways. He laughed, "like you were drunk or something."

"Boy? I'm just really tired today." I said.

The word I was most focused on in everything he said to me was, "we." The Lawsons were a large family, Mama, Daddy and six kids. Plus, Karla senior, their Mother, was very close to my Mother. How much had they seen? How much had they speculated? How long would it be before Mrs. Lawson would make her way to my Mom to let her know what she saw? How many other leads had I left uncovered last night? What am I going to do when she finds out I gave money to a drag queen, me and Wexler.. together at a gay bar? Paranoia had set in, and I could NOT let them find out I was gay. MISTER GALLOWS WAS GOING TO HAVE TO DIE!

Church went on and there was no sign of Wexler. I don't even think Scheidler preached that day either. That day was all very much a blur, but from what I recall it went on not much different than any other Sunday. We'd go home to eat, nap then back up and out the door at 6:30 to do it all over again Sunday night. Except for the Sundays that Scheidler and I spent in his office, Sundays all seemed pretty much the same. When Scheidler and my interactions became more frequent, each Sunday just seemed to run together.

This one particular Sunday was however very different. I had fallen asleep Saturday night after giving my privates a good illicit working over. I had forgotten to slip my gay porn magazine back under my mattress.
"Ferron?" Mom was opening the door. Ferron dear it's time to get up and get ready for chur…

There was the magazine laying on the floor wide open to my favorite page. She picked it up and looked for not even a second and then dropped it back to the floor. She came over to my bedside and slowly started to pull my covers back. When I clutched at the covers she knew everything she was trying to find out. She turned and walked out of the room.

"Mom... mom wait."

"Why Ferron, why, Will!" She called out for my dad.

A few minutes later my Dad came into the room and demanded the magazine from me. He didn't say anything else. He just took it and left. There was no conversation at breakfast or the ride to church or the ride back. When I got home Dad summoned me to the backyard. When I got there, Dad my brother, and I were the only ones at this meeting.

Dad brought a shovel and some lighter fluid. I thought. "Oh shit, he's going to kill me and just dispose of my body right here in the backyard." He threw my magazine on the ground.

"This mess is not allowed in my house." He said sternly. I wanted your brother to be here so he would know exactly who he was living with." Dad didn't know, because I had never told anyone, that my brother's dick was the first one that was ever in my mouth. He told me to dig a hole with the shovel. Then I had to gather kindling. I was to light a fire and go through the magazine page by page and say "I renounce the devil" as I threw each page into the fire. This particular rite of passage certainly was not as fun as the naked dancing one. Dad closed in prayer and I was told to cover the hole now with the loose dirt. After that, I was under a rule that I could not be in any rooms of the house alone behind closed doors for longer than 5 minutes. If I was caught I would get a whoopin. Needless to say, I got several whoopins. The whoopins only stopped after that one time he came to beat me and I started screaming "Yes Daddy, do it again." He just dropped the belt and left.

It was now graduation season and my brother was graduating from Bible School at Jesus International Bible College in Dallas Texas. He had been away from the family for some time as a result of some behavioral problems at home. He went to stay with Uncle Alphie in Florida for a while and subsequently ended up making a decision to attend Bible school in Dallas after he got himself "straightened out."

We were taking a family road trip to Dallas to participate in the ceremony. I hadn't seen or spoken to Craig for several years but I remembered that Dallas was where he had moved to. I decided I was going to try and find a way to look him up when I got there. I wanted to see my friend and of course I wanted to see if we could have the chance to travel space together one more time for old time sake.

I for one was not a fan of road trips with the family. I really just tried to sleep through the whole thing but Dad insisted on always waking me and trying to teach me, to no avail, how to read the road atlas map. He would also wake me up just to say "we're almost there" when we in fact were not.

When we finally did get into Dallas and settled in the accommodations the school provided, I took a minute to slip away to a pay phone and I started combing through the local phonebook trying to find every Bannister listing I could, and I called every single one looking for Craig. No Hits. Then I called 411 and asked the operator to search for Craig Bannister Sr., That was his Dad. She gave me a number that was not in the phonebook. I called and a female voice answered.

"Hello?" it was Craig's older sister Laura.
"Hi is Craig there? Craig Jr.?"
"Yeah hold on who is this?"
"This is Ferron Wiley, Im a Friend of Craig's from Roches..."

"CRAIG.. PHONE FOR YOU!" she yelled off in the distance.

"Hello?" Craig said coming to the phone.

"Hey Man how you doin?" I said smiling.

:" Hey who is this?"

"Craig its Ferron from Rochester."

"For Real? Man How are you?"

"I'm good. Good to hear your voice. I'm here in Dallas, my brother is graduating tomorrow from Jesus international.."

"What, really?! My sister is a student there, she graduates tomorrow too."

"O Snap so you gonna be here tomorrow, we gotta try and find each other!"

"Yeah I know it would be great to see you," he said.

It seemed like we got to talk a really long time before my quarter ran out and we had to hang up. I was so freakin excited and I felt so accomplished. I could barely sleep thinking about Craig and what might jump off between us the next day.

Finally, that boring ass ceremony was over and I started scanning the crowd with my rated x-ray vision trying to spot Craig. I recognized Laura from when they called her name to come to get her diploma so I focused on her. I figured the rest of her family would make their way to her. I was right, I spotted Craig wearing a suit giving his sister a congratulatory hug. I told my brother "Good Job," shook his hand and I started making a beeline through the crowd toward Craig.

When I reached him he smiled and reached his hand out for mine for a handshake.

"Hey man, good to see you."

His handshake was firm but his skin was very soft.

It's good to see you too, Craig. I said slightly moving in closer letting people by behind me.

We made some small talk for a minute or so and finally I said,
Hey I am staying in one of the vacant dorms here on campus there is
a Denny's right next door, we can grab something to eat and hang out
at my room and we can catch up."
'Ok well let me see what my family is doing."

Well, it turned out that Craig was free and we did meet at the Denny's.
Of course, I had been there already for an hour pining. I stepped into
the bathroom to get rid of some of the coffee I was rebelliously
drinking and not too long after that Craig walked in the bathroom and
went to the open urinal next to me. I instantly got hard as a rock
thinking "oh shit is this going to happen right here, just like when we
were in Jr. high school?"

You got us a table already? Craig said as he peed.
"Uh, Yeah I did," I said. All I could think about was the first time I ever
saw Craig's dick. How big it was, how much he came, all while
listening to his piss splatter heavily in the back of the urinal.

And then, ZIIIPP! Craig fastened himself up.
"Let's eat man." Craig said.
"Sure." I said, trying to shove my hardon back into my pants and calm
down.

Craig and I had a quick bite to eat and we chatted about old times at
school but he didn't breathe a word about how we used to hit it.
Eventually, I did convince him to come up to my room and chill for a
while.

When we started running out of things to talk about, I finally tried to
shift gears and move in. I wanted him so bad right now. I reached out

and started unbuttoning Craig's shirt and pulling it out from his belted pants. I ran my lips over his left nipple and he panted inhaling with pleasure. I ran my hand between his legs and felt that monster and I immediately went into high gear. I had just gotten his belt undone and pants unzipped when I could hear Craig mumbling something under his breath, mumbling, mumbling but he was getting louder and clearer.

"Now the works of the flesh are manifest, which are these; Adultery, fornication, uncleanness, lasciviousness, Craig said pulling himself out from under me and beginning to refasten his pants.

"Idolatry, witchcraft, hatred, variance, emulations, wrath, strife, seditions, heresies, Envyings, murders, drunkenness, revellings, and such like: of the which I tell you before, as I have also told you in time past, that they which do such things shall not inherit the kingdom of God." He continued in an almost robotic tone and buttoning his shirt.

Ferron, this is not who I am anymore', he said looking straight ahead, not making eye contact.

"What do you mean anymore? You're Craig, my buddy from Jr. high school the guy whose dick I loved to suck, my sci-fi road dog."

"Yeah, but we can't do THIS anymore. I don't want to miss heaven."

"You seemed like you were pretty close to heaven a minute ago?"

" I think I better go."

"So we don't cum?" I asked.

" Oh shit.. I mortify therefore my members which are upon the earth; fornication, uncleanness, inordinate affection, evil concupiscence, and covetousness, which is idolatry. He said, frantically restraining himself and gathering his jacket.

He was breathing heavily. Clearly being in the bible belt all these years, it was like Craig had become one of those pod people from Invasion of the body snatchers, some kind of evangelical zombie. It was like he was a shell of himself and his insides had been replaced. But whatever he had been reprogrammed with, in this moment, it was not taking and he was about to short circuit like that square dancing fem-bot in that remake of The Stepford Wives.

Eventually, I gave in. I put my hand on his shoulder and walked him to the elevator. I rode down with him because I had a feeling this was going to be the last time I ever saw him so, I wanted to savor the moment.

"I'm good here man. Nice to see you again for the most part." He said anxiously. I'm just gonna call my mom to come get me I'll wait here at the Denny's"

"Ok then Craig. I'm glad I got to see you too." I watched him walk away to the Denny's and I returned to the elevator and went back to my room. I then immediately found and made use of my travel bottle of lotion.

CHAPTER 12

The burden of the secrets of what had transpired between Scheidler and I had become overwhelming to me. Bits and pieces were slipping out to my friends and rumors were starting to fly. Things were getting back to Scheidler and he was beginning to panic. He began to retaliate, refuting the story saying I was a pathological liar and my school records proved it. One Friday night I was pulled aside by the youth leader at the time, her name was Patra. I told her I thought Scheidler was acting strangely toward me. She told me that she knew something was going on and that I should not worry that God was going to work everything out. At that moment Scheidler passed us in the foyer, glared angrily at me and said, you better watch who you're talking to and what you're saying! As he spoke he just kept walking into another back office.

"Did you see that?" I said.
Yes... I saw it and I heard it. Patra said with a disheartened expression on her face.

Scheidler sat on the board of directors at God's Mountain Bible University where Al, Larry Greenhouse, Weighton Tabernacle's music minister, and Pete Reddings whom I think today is now the Pastor of Weighton Tabernacle all attended Bible School. Weighton Tabernacle often encouraged their high school students to attend God's Mountain if they had not made any definitive continued education plans. Vaughn and Karla had already gone off to God's Mountain last semester. After I was not allowed to return to Christlight, Scheidler probably feeling very uncomfortable having me around offered me a guaranteed acceptance to God's Mountain.

"It would be a great situation for you." He said. "You will have some time on your own, away from Mom and Dad and you will be in a Christian environment so Mom and Dad will be at ease too." He said.

The idea was appealing to me and I was really missing Vaughn. So I talked it up with Mom and Dad and eventually, they were in agreement. I would be off to God's Mountain Bible University on the next semester.

With the unrest at church and rumors flying. Mom had had it she wanted to get to the bottom of what was going on with me. What was causing all the delinquency, the sex, the defiance, and rebellion? Frustrated that nothing was working for me she compassionately cornered me in the basement just steps away from where I had first asked God into my life.

Things were already happening with regard to my relationship with my mother. My heart was softening to the fact of how much it hurt her when I lied to her. I decided at one point before this meeting internally that I would never lie to my mother again. I decided no matter how deceitful or mischievous I had been, I would not lie about it. I would own my own actions. It didn't mean I wasn't going to be deceitful or mischievous anymore it just meant I wasn't going to lie about it. As my mother probed, her eyes began to fill with tears at my silence. I was not ready to bring my mother's whole world down. We wrestled silently with each other for what seemed to be like hours… until I found the courage and the words to tearfully tell her about Scheidler and me. She did not cry in front of me. She just kept asking me questions while I was on a roll. Later I remember her telling me her reaction was that she wanted to scream. When I finished she told me to stay in the basement while she went upstairs. I think she went to call my Dad. Dad didn't believe me, he told me as much. But after further investigation of his own, he found that I may not have been Scheidler's only victim. It wasn't until then, that he said he believed me.

A few weeks had passed, Scheidler had finished preaching and service was over. All the elders, deacons and Weighton Tabernacles top church officials were summoned into Scheidler's office. They were in there for a while. Normally our family would have been gone by now. The church maintenance man was in vacuuming the sanctuary while I sat on the back row pew just outside Scheidler's office. After some time I was called into the office. I moved past what seemed to be all the large figures standing in the room, to the center of the room. If I had to guess there were maybe 20 people in that room. That same room. Scheidler was sitting at his desk with his head down, not looking at anyone. I don't remember exactly who it was but someone said,

"Your father has brought some accusations to the board of Elders on your behalf and as a part of the investigation, we need to hear from you that these accusations are true. I am going to ask you some questions and I just need you to answer yes or no, okay? I just nodded my head yes.

Have you spent time here in the office with Pastor Scheidler after school hours?
"Yes," I replied.
My mind was going in and out as he asked the questions, I didn't want to be there. Some questions were being asked and I do not remember answering them, I was on autopilot, I was detaching.
"Did Pastor Scheidler engage in inappropriate sexual acts with you during these times?"
"Yes," I replied.
"Oh, God... Jesus!" Scheidler wept from his part sitting, part prone position on the desk. When it was over they requested that I not speak of these issues to anyone else while the investigation was being conducted. I agreed and I was dismissed from the room.

Ermaline, Scheidler's wife had assumed the role of interim Pastor during the course of the investigation. There were times when she would say things from the pulpit during her altar calls that I just knew were directed at me, just to make me feel guilty about speaking up about her husband. The church was split right down the middle. I was riddled with guilt and shame, I wanted to kill myself but apparently, according to what I had learned in Weighton Tabernacles catechism classes, suicide was a sin that would definitely end me up burning in hell. So it would be better to take my chances and live and hopefully one day just be delivered from homosexuality.

I would try to go to the altar and pray and seek God. Altar workers would come and whisper in my ear telling me that God wasn't going to answer my prayers until I told the truth about Pastor Scheidler. That all liars have their place in the pit of Hell.

Sister Sara Leanne Reddings was the Senior Elder at the time. It was believed that she held more clout in the church than anyone, despite the fact that she was not the pastor. She was the daughter of Thomas McPhea the original founder of. Weighton Assemblies of God before the church's name was changed to Weighton Tabernacle some years after his passing. Sister Reddings scheduled an interview with me as a part of the investigation to get clarity on the details of what had transpired between Scheidler and me. She met with my Mom first while I sat outside the conference room. After a while, she called me into the room and Mom and I traded places.

Sister Reddings talked with me for a while either to put me, or perhaps herself at ease, but her facial expressions became more and more disturbed as I described to her the particulars of Scheidler and my encounters. Finally, at the end of our discussion, she closed her book of notes and folded her hands across it. She thanked me for coming and her face began to redden, tears began to come from the sides of her eyes. Squeezing them tightly shut, she put her hands on mine and she said, "This is a lot of information to sort out, and if what you are saying is true, I'm sorry,I am deeply, deeply sorry that this happened." She began to weep more intensely. I was crying too.

Things were quiet for several weeks until there was an announcement made that there would be an all-church meeting to notify the Church of the outcomes of the investigation and the fate of Scheidler's position as Pastor. I made a point to be there because it had been a while since I had heard anything. It frustrated me that things were out of my hands now, that I did not have the power anymore. It bothered me that decisions were being made about things that affected my life and suddenly I was the one with the least information. All they said in the meeting was that Harold Scheidler had been asked to resign as

Pastor and that the position of Pastor would temporarily be filled by Sister Reddings. Now I was more than pissed. I was pissed off that they would not take a stand on either side whether the allegations were true or not. The other family in the church that came forward with allegations was also black. I often wondered if that was the reason why they would never confirm or deny the allegations. Maybe they did not want to take the risk, thinking we might have collaborated. I felt like okay, on one hand, the church was supporting me but it became apparent to me that when it came down to choosing between standing with me or protecting their own interest, I would definitely be sitting on the back pew.

CHAPTER 13

Church attendance had dropped off significantly as supporters of
Scheidler made an exodus. Some stayed around I think just to make
life hell for me. I think my parents were experiencing the same. Albeit I
was still on my way to Bible School in a few weeks and would soon be
out of Rochester, I would not have to deal with all of this anymore. It
was over finally, so I thought.

Dad decided since I would be leaving home for the first time it was
time to talk about life. He pulled me aside one day while we were
cutting the grass together and told me that he noticed that I seem to
gravitate toward homosexuality, that I hung around situations and
people that if nothing else gave the appearance that they were
homosexual. He told me in his fatherly wisdom that from now on if I
encountered homosexuals in my life who expressed an interest in
having sex with me that it was okay for me to punch them in the face.
"I don't care if it is on the street, at work, or at bible school you have
my permission to punch them in the face."

I realize that he most likely was responding to the feelings he may have been having knowing his son had been sexually abused, but at this particular juncture in my life, I'm thankful for the disobedient streak that was in me as this story would probably have a very different ending, or perhaps would not ever even be told if I had followed my Dad's counsel from that day. Sadly, I did not know my Father well enough to know if he was just sad and angry about me, or if he actually believed it was ok to assault people. Unfortunately, Dad never talked much about his feelings, so based on my experiences with him I can only assume the latter was true.

Vaughn and Karla were back for the summer and we made plans for the three of us to drive back to school at God's Mountain together. On the way there I prayed to God for the forgiveness of my sins up to this point.
"God, I'm sorry for messing everything up. I'm sorry for being such a rotten person. God, I want to turn over a new leaf. I want to go to God's Mountain and learn what I need to know to do your will the right way. I'm not going to ignore my studies like in the past I promise God. I just want you and everybody else to be happy with me. I don't want to be the cause of any more pain."

When I arrived at God's Mountain it was not very different than being at Weighton Tabernacle. I already knew a lot of people there. It was not home however with regard to the food. To me, it was like they figured if Paul the Apostle could eat locusts then I guess we would be just fine with whatever swill of the day they slopped out.

My first day of orientation the most exciting thing I found to eat was from a large box of frosted donuts that were left out for students to grab. So I grabbed a few and thought, "this will carry me over to lunchtime, maybe lunch would be better, Yeah." But biting into one of the donuts I realized it was more than a day old. It tasted like months old. It literally fell apart in my mouth! I started feverishly spitting the crumbs out onto the sidewalk. "Damn you, Scheidler!" I thought. "This ain't even right," I said.

Some upperclassmen had warned me somewhat about God's Mountain's conservative approaches to Christianity, That meant that there were some clear lines that had been drawn that's separated their ideas apart from any of the soulful black Christian experiences I aspired to. One morning while participating in a class on worship, I was asked to open the class in the hymn Have Thine Own Way from the piano. When I sat down to play, some of the other black students in the class were in the back waving their hands, shaking their heads and mouthing the words, "don't do it, don't do it." Of course my innate nature to rock the boat took over and I began to sing the song with all the sounds of blackness that I could muster. I could see the hands that were earlier waving caution to me, now covering their faces and giggled expressions of "Well thank ya God!" Coming from behind them. When I was done the instructor thanked me with a tight-lipped expression and I sat back down in the second row as he just went on with his presentation. I thought to myself, "Lord where am I?"

Pete Reddings had called an impromptu prayer meeting with all the students who were from Weighton Tabernacle to pray about everything that was happening back home. The prayers went up but I could not muster up any particular love in my heart for Weighton Tabernacle at the time. At the close of the prayer session, while everyone was standing there in a meditative state as if waiting to hear from God, I backed myself away to go be alone, and cry. I couldn't help feeling like these particular prayers would not have to be made if it weren't for me.

Over the next few days, I continued to try and honor my promise to God. I was attending classes but, as usual, was totally lost in all of them. Inevitably I began to lose interest and started falling into old habits. I started being late for classes and again I wasn't taking things seriously.

Two weeks into my term, I found a note on my dorm room door summoning me to the Dean's office. I started to panic and I thought "My God I am being put out already." I started getting all my words together so I could be apologetic for not being on time to classes and create the atmosphere for sympathy. I asked another student where the Dean's office was because I hadn't even been on campus long enough to know that. I went into the building. This building looked as if it had been an old church itself with its sculpted, high vaulted ceilings. My appointment was at 2 p.m. No one was around. I sat in the lobby for a while and then maybe an hour later someone came to the top of the stairs and said,
"Are you Ferron Wiley?"
"Yes," I replied smiling.
"Okay, someone will be with you shortly." She said. As she disappeared back upstairs.
I waited, and waited, and waited, 6 p.m. and nothing.
"My God it never took this long for me to get kicked out of anything else before," I thought.
Finally 6:30 p.m.
"Mr. Wiley the Dean is ready for you now."
I started making my way up the long staircase to the Dean's office. He was on the phone and he motioned for me to sit down. There were two other women in the room with us, one being the woman who greeted me at the steps. When the Dean got off the phone he introduced himself and asked if I knew why I was here. I started to

rattle off my prepared speech on how sorry I was for missing classes and my action plan for improvement. He said that all that was admirable, but he needed to discuss something with me and he informed me that it would be necessary for our conversation to be recorded to preserve authenticity. As he said this, the woman nearest the tape recorder pressed the record buttons.

"What brought you to God's Mountain Ferron?" The Dean asked.

"Well I hadn't really made any plans for college and I thought this would be a good foundational transition time while I made up my mind," I said.

You realize that there are some things going on in your church back home that has left a lot of unanswered questions?" He asked.

"Yeah, I guess so. I replied, my heart sinking. I just thought it was all over now. I said. I just thought maybe coming to God's Mountain was a chance for me to move on."

"As we have become aware of certain information it looks as though your term at God's Mountain will have to be discontinued." The Dean said.

"Please, not again. Is there anything we can work out?" I said. But just then something inside me shut down and said, "fuck it, don't say another word."

"Ferron, we feel that in light of the circumstances it would be best for you to go back home until these matters are resolved and maybe apply again in the spring."

"How long do I have?" I asked, disgusted.

"We would like to have this resolved by Monday." He said.

It was already Thursday. I had to call my parents that night, explain to them that I have already been expelled from Bible School, ask them to try and arrange a bus ticket, say goodbye to all my friends new and old, pack all my stuff and be out by the following Monday.

Pete Reddings took me and my huge taped up box of stuff to the Trailways bus station that Monday morning. He hugged me goodbye and said, "hang in there."

I rode the bus for the long journey home. I had to transfer to another bus in Boston which meant somehow I was going to have to push that huge taped box through the long terminal to get to the next bus. Predictably, as the formula of my life would have it no other way, the luggage handler's removed my box from the undercarriage and it busted open when they dropped it on the ground. So I dragged the tattered box about halfway until I exhausted myself and again said "fuck it." I just left the whole thing right there in the corridor so I wouldn't miss my connection.

CHAPTER 14

I was back at home in Rochester now and was faced with what I was now going to do with my life. That thought stream didn't last long when Dad told me that if I was going to be living at home I would have to contribute to help pay expenses, so I was off to find a job.

Pittsville Ponds Atrium turned out to be the jackpot for me evidently because I started working at the Scrantom's stationery store not steps away from where Edward's department store used to be. I got the job as a stock boy. I did inventory ordering and pricing. I was getting along pretty well when one day as I was putting out some merchandise I was approached by a short blonde-haired woman in her floor-length wool coat carrying her leather briefcase. She was well-dressed and her hair was cut and one of those business-like blunted shoulder-length styles, kind of like how Susan Dey wore hers in that TV show LA Law. Who knows maybe she was copying it on purpose.
"Are you Ferron Wiley?" She asked in a low tone.
"Why?" I said hesitantly and continuing to work.

"I'm with the District Attorney's office and I wondered if when you have some time we could talk?"

"What about?" I said.

"It's about Harold Scheidler." She said.

"Look I really want to be done with all that," I said.

"I can understand that, but the state of New York is working on an indictment against him and we really need your testimony."

"How did you find me?"

"Standard investigative procedures it wasn't difficult, look I realize you're working right now do you think we could talk on your break?"

'Can I think about it?'

'Absolutely, here's my card you be sure to call me when you're ready. Just keep in mind that we're working with a statute of limitations so don't take too long."

I took the card, she turned and sort of bounced as she walked toward the front of the store.

My name was mud at Weighton Tabernacle, there were more victims and I had heard that Scheidler had started another church with his followers who left Weighton. Scheidler had made me out to be a liar after my oath to God and myself that I would not have that to be a part of my identity anymore. Kicked out of school after school, my life was all screwed up in my eyes beyond repair, and this fool was going on with his like nothing ever happened. "Oh Hells no!"

The next day I called the district attorney and scheduled for a lunch meeting of which she was to pay for. I picked the Vineyard, one of the nicer restaurants in the area, and not far from my job. I was bound and determined that I was going to get something out of all of this. I ordered and ate everything I could on the menu that day. As I ate, I again disclosed the events of the encounters I had with Scheidler to her and gave detailed answers to her questions. The more questions she asked, the more food I ordered. As a sense of release, contentment, and satisfaction came over me, my appetites were having a Hay-day. The fulfillment I experienced. The combination of food consumption and the opportunity to exact my vengeance was very satisfying to me but also very mentally debilitating. For years after this, I would wrestle with my weight, my self-esteem, and my relationships with others as a result of the connections I was making with those feelings that day.

CHAPTER 15

Former Pastor of Weighton Tabernacle Church in Weighton Howard J Scheidler was arrested today on several counts of indecency with a minor and child endangerment charges. The clergyman who recently began leading another church in Greece, New York shortly after his resignation from Weighton Tabernacle, is behind bars tonight pending the outcome of allegations that he engaged sexually with underage boys that attended the Weighton church, Broadcasted the news reporter. It wasn't long before pictures with my face blurred out were on the screen and I was being referred to as the minor. Weighton Tabernacle, I am sure, was not happy that the church's name was in the news again under bad publicity.

I never was quite sure whether it was God's hand or my Dad's that was moving but nevertheless, I think Mom began to feel the sting at church and it wasn't long before Dad had a transfer on his job to California and the Wiley's were getting out of Dodge.

I decided however that I wasn't going anywhere. I wasn't going to miss this opportunity to make a go of it on my own. I had already gone through more rough spots than most people my age I felt or, had I? I was big and bad enough to go it alone. I felt like I was alone most of the time anyway. Yeah, California sounded nice but I certainly did not feel like moving all the way across the country with my family. No way! So I saved my money from my job at Scrantom's and found me a place. It was a tiny one-bedroom love shack and it was on the same road as my job, so I would only have to catch one bus back and forth to go to work.

When the day came for me to move in though, you would have thought I had stabbed my mother in the heart. We sat together with Dad and chatted for a while, to see if there were any unresolved issues I guess. Obviously, there were plenty, but there wasn't enough time to cover them now. She just sat there crying and looking at me saying "it isn't right, it just isn't right." As if to say this is not the way it's supposed to happen. I will never forget the look of anguish on her face when Dad and I pulled out of the driveway with the last of the things they gave me to get started.

We drove down the road in silence. When we got to my place, Dad helped me in with my stuff. When we were done he prayed over me for protection and guidance as I started the journey of life on my own. He hugged me and we said our goodbyes.

When the door closed behind him and I heard his car pull off, I 'bout did a couple of cartwheels and a pirouette in my living room. I was screeching "FREE... I'M FREE" and twirling about my apartment until (ploomp) I fell out, out of breath. I zipped around putting things into place as quickly as I could because I remembered that happy hour at the Liberty was only a few hours away. I was not about to miss two-for-one well-drinks and now that I was within walking distance? Chyle, please! It was my first day grown!

I heard someone once say that you are only grown the day you become responsible for your own foolishness. I didn't even know how to get my phone turned on or even that lights had to be paid for, but I'll be damned if I was going to miss going out to the club and for the first time not having to be held accountable to anyone!

It was Wednesday night about 9 or so and the Liberty was just on the verge of filling up with the midweek crowd. I was standing at one of the table islands sipping on my rum and coke watching the video screen embedded in the center of the table when, Glenn, came around the corner from the Dance Floor. He was a tall, white, husky, grand old girl with his eyebrows arched so perfectly it almost made me want to go to McDonald's for a hamburger. He for some reason fancied carrying himself in a manner that called to mind Alexis Colby from the TV show Dynasty.

I was turning to leave my post at the table and we nearly ran right into each other. Squinting our eyes, pouting our lips with our hands on our hips we slowly and cattily stared each other down and sized each other up. Finally, I decided to break our little choreography.

"So, what are you all about anyway?" I asked in an accusatory tone. And who might you be? Glen replied in his best Patricia Neal voice, his eyes even shiftier now.
You know, there's nothing ruder than answering a question with a question my dear. I said.
Don't question me Mary!! Don't you realize I could crush you with a single phone call? He said upping his cattiness and transforming his character from Patricia Neal to Erica from All My Children.

"Curb trash! that's all you are darling, curb trash!" he grandly pronounced.

"From Trailer Trash to lounge lizard there's no telling what they'll come up with next!" we both said simultaneously, laughing hysterically as we recited the all too familiar lines from Dynasty.

"Oh, I like you," Glenn's the name and you are? He said.
"I'm Ferron," I replied lightening up a bit.
Suddenly the intro to Never Gonna Give You Up by Rick Astley began to Boom over the Dance Floor.
"Shit, this is my favorite song, Come Dance With Me!" Glen said rushing to the floor. Glenn got on the floor doing some crazy white boy dance, and I joined best I could. I thought to myself, hmm a new friend, well we'll see how this goes.

There were a few drag performances between the dance breaks and even a live performance by Michael Lee. Mike was tall muscly black guy was revered as the big black stud of the house at the Liberty. He was always scantily dressed to show off his body. Mike was always picked to be the sexy backup dancer for a number of the drag queen numbers.

Tonight Mike was endeavoring to showcase his talent for singing. Mike and Tim his keyboard player came onto the stage and Tim started to play the pop sounding original dance number. Mike grabbed the microphone and began to dance about the stage as people started getting into the song as well as some of Mike's sexy moves. However everyone's enthusiasm came to a grinding halt when Mike opened his mouth to sing. Everyone just stood there with arms crossed and holding their drinks in kind of a catatonic side eyed glance as they endured the performance. I felt so bad for him because I remember how I felt not being counted among the best singers at church, but this sound was kin to what you might hear when cats in heat are fighting in the alley. Even I wasn't this bad.

When it was finally over the dance floor music resumed amidst some sympathetic applause and Mike came off the stage and made his way to the guy who I assume was his lover. His lover was an even more physically fit, body boomin dark skinned black guy who I noticed most times just standing off in the shadows by himself until some hot song came on and Mike dragged him to the dance floor so they could dance together. They exchanged some conversation that I couldn't make out but if I were to guess, it appeared that Mike's lover wasn't very impressed with Mike's performance either and wasn't afraid to say it.

At the end of a few songs on the dance floor, the lights went down low and the classic piano intro to I Will Survive rang out over the speakers. As Gloria Gaynor's voice began to sing the famous lyrics, the lights on the stage burst on. The curtain flung open to reveal none other than, Falexis!

Falexis, the often ridiculed, not so popular but still managed to be a regular occurrence at the Liberty female impersonator. Tonight she was dressed to be a mess, in a dress she had tried to make herself. However, Falexis's body dimensions were putting it politely, an oddity and the nightmare even for the best of designers. Her ensemble was made complete by the tape on her horn rim Coke bottle lens glasses, and a poor decision to use her own hair that looked as if it had not been washed in days, instead of a wig. She kind of reminded me of Rick the nerdy guy from my junior high days if he had gone on to Fashion Diva school but didn't study very hard.

As her performance progressed, Boos, heckles and mockery could be heard from the crowd. Then the room filled with hysterical howels as Falexis attempt to gracefully swing around a pole on the stage ended up with her sliding off the front of the stage into some nearby tables and a horrendous crash! Of course, the DJ couldn't resist ending the performance making that sound of the needle scratching across the record just to add his own messy accent to the already tragic scene

Falexis fumbled around on the floor for a bit trying to find her glasses and grabbing herself together ran off backstage humiliated as the DJ played loud siren noises from the booth like they did on Showtime at the Apollo when the Sandman came running out.

Glenn just put one finger to his mouth and said "hmmm."
Although I did laugh at the whole incident, I felt bad for Falexis. She was giving it her all and no one appreciated it. I have always had a soft spot for the underdog. "
You think she's okay?" I asked Glenn.

Oh don't worry about that girl, every week it's the same thing. She gets up there and she gets worse every time, it's all that damn drinking she does.

Soon the music began to jump again and my attention was diverted from Falexis's peril to all the boys that were now in the club. It would be last call before you know it, so of course, I wasted no time making my way to find me a companion for the night.

I wasn't having any luck and had gotten pretty tipsy so I started getting ready to leave when Glenn came bounding around the corner again this time with Falexis and he asked me if I needed a ride home. I said, 'sure.' because I really was not up for the walk home.

Glen, Falexis and I piled into Glen's fire engine red 1986 Ford Escort GT and we sped off down the road toward my place.

When we got there we all climbed out of the car and went up the back stairs to my apartment. We sat around for a while laughing about the night and talking about boys. Falexis, drunker than all of us eventually passed out in my living room floor. I had to get up early to go to work so I started motioning to Glen to get Falexis up and take her home because I needed to go to sleep.

"Honey, I can't take her with me, I live in Mendon," Glen said. Well, she can't stay here Mary. I have to work in the morning."

"Oh, Just let her sleep here and put her out in the morning," Glen said.

"Oh no, you brought her here you take her where she needs to go."

"Honey, she lives in the shelter, and I don't know where it is." Glen snapped.

Just then, Falexis raised his head long enough to giggle and say, "and I can't go to the shelter, I'm too drunk and they won't let me in." Then he fell face-first back into the carpet.

Glenn and I looked at each other

"Oh, well, honey I got to get going myself."

Oh no you don't you are not leaving him here with me!"

"Honey, she'll be fine, she'll be laying just as you see her now when you wake up." Glen said as he moved toward the door,

" Just wake her up when you leave for work and tell her she has to go. Okay, honey? Trust me she'll be fine. Ta-ta."

"GLEN!" I yelled. The door slammed shut

Falexis laid there on my living room floor face in the carpet snoring. I just said forget it and let her lay there. I went to my room and closed the door and went to sleep.

I got up for work the next day and there was Falexis still laying on the floor only He wasn't still face first in the carpet. He was nestled up in a fetal position resting comfortably. The redness of his face had subsided and he looked content.

As I just stood there staring at him I began to have a moment. I wondered what he might be dreaming about, I wondered where his family was. I wondered where he was going to end up tonight. I started seeing him as a person instead of a drunk bungling drag queen that people laughed at all the time.

None the less he could not stay here while I was gone, so I started nudging him to wake up. When he came to, he looked around the room with a kind of comical crazy looking twist on his face. He stretched his arms way above his head until his belly button showed and he yawned like a little kid. "..Mmph this was really nice, I really enjoyed myself." He said. "But I really have to be going, we should do this again sometime." He said as if he were just leaving a ladies luncheon or worse as if we had just slept together.

"Uh, ok?" I said puzzled. "So I guess I'll see you at the club again?" I asked.

"Yeah that's for sure!" he replied in a "rock on" tone. Ok well, have a good one." "Byieee"

Falexis meandered down the road and ... " Shit!" I'm late for work!"

CHAPTER 16

The months went on. Dad and Mom, My brother, and even my Grandmother who had been living in Rochester had moved on to California. My sister had gotten married, had a child, and was in the process of divorce while so much was going on with me. She was living in New York City now raising her son. I was the only one left. I wasn't attending church anymore. All the things that had happened at Weighton Tabernacle had left a very sour taste in my mouth toward Church, and God. I didn't want anything to do with a God that let the kinds of things that happened to me, happen at all. Christianity made absolutely no sense to me. As far as I was concerned it was all a fake, a *money-making* scheme and I was even angrier that no one was letting me in on it.

If living *for* God *m*ade such a big difference then why were all the "sinners" living such happy lives, and I was so miserable? I mean in my heart I wasn't living against God as much as I **just** wanted to be happy, but it seemed the more I tried the worse I was at it.

I was convinced that God had it out for me and I didn't know what it was he wanted from *me*. I mean I had prayed the sinner's prayer I even went down the aisle at Weighton Tabernacle so they *could* teach me how to speak in tongues. I even got slain in the Spirit a couple of *time*s and laid on the floor to let God "work" on me. What was so wrong with me that I cou*l*dn't be happy like ev*ery*one else?

*T*he *m*essage had been drilled hard and long into me that as long as I was gay there was no h*ope* f*or me* to ever be in fellowship with God, and that all of the turmoil I was experiencing in my *life* was God trying to get my attention, chastening me so I would turn from my wicked *ways, r*epent. Then and only then would **He** bless me like He blesses all those that do h*is* wi*ll.*

But no matter how hard I tried I couldn't change myself. I thought maybe my faith wasn't s*trong* enough. But they took that crutch away from me too with that scripture "God has *g*iven to *e*very man the measure of faith, and if I had but the faith of a mustard seed I *c*ould *mo*v*e* this mountain."

So since I had confessed my sin and I had the faith why wasn't I changing?

Oh yeah, that's It I have a demonic spirit of rebellion operating in my life and I needed to go through a prayer line and throw up in a bucket until the demon was gone and then I would be free to fight the devil and the sin of homosexuality. So after all the prayer lines, I decided Ok God it's you and me your word says that if I ask anything according to your will it will be granted unto me, "If being gay is not of you then take it from me, change me, God! Create in me a clean heart that I might do your will, God please can't you hear me!"

And God was just as silent as he was on my 16th Birthday > < and on my way to Bible school and all the other times I prayed this fervently. I could not understand why God would not speak to me like everyone else who says they hear from God every day. So I assumed God had chosen to ignore me or that I must just be one of those people predestined for hell. God was never going to answer me. Ever.

It was then I decided that if I was going to hell anyway, baby I was going to make it count while am here on earth. If I was going to hell for something I had no control over, then I might as well go for a good reason. If God had rejected me, then I reject God too along with everyone that represents him. In fact, as far as I am concerned you don't even exist. We can put you right on the shelf with Santa Claus, The Easter Bunny, and the Tooth Fairy. childhood idols.

There were those things that nagged me though that I had attributed to my belief that God was real. Like when I tried everything to get a wart off my hand. It wouldn't go away. I used Compound W, even tried to chew it off because it was so irritating and embarrassing. One day Mom after attempting to dig the root out with a needle she sterilized by holding it under the flame of a match and then cleaning with a cotton ball soaked in rubbing alcohol, She prayed over the wart and told me to go wash in the sink 7 times like the lepers in the bible and, miraculously, it disappeared within a week and my thumb where the wart was, was like baby skin.

There was the time when we had a mouse in the house and it seems that we had no luck catching it. It was getting into everything. Dad prayed and bound up vermin in the house and the next day the mouse's head was finally caught in one of the many traps that had been set for weeks

Still, this did not explain why GOD was not answering MY prayers. So I was pretty much done. It wasn't because I wanted to. I wanted to love God and feel like he loved me like everyone else around me. As far as I was concerned I had been tricked by Christianity and there was no telling if there was any truth in it at all. It wasn't even the idea of God I hated so much, it was Christianity and Christians I couldn't stand. You see Christianity had taught me one thing, and that was how to hate, and I really needed somewhere to vent all the hate I had in me.

I couldn't hate God because I might go to hell. I couldn't hate other people because the bible says if I don't love people I can't say I love God. Strangely enough, I hadn't found anything in the bible against hating myself. In fact, it kinda goes out of its way to encourage you to put yourself last. So in an endeavor to garner whatever acceptance from God that I could, I became an imitator of God and made myself the target of my own wrath, and exact my rage I did. I tried to consciously and systematically ruin every chance I had at living a successful or healthy life. If God was at all about preserving my life or keeping me safe I would make him work overtime, or I would make it very easy for him to take me out.

Not wearing proper clothing in the cold, hoping to get pneumonia, choosing not to wear a seatbelt anytime I rode in a vehicle, just so I would be sure to be thrown through the windshield in the event there was an accident. Binge drinking, unsafe sex, bathhouses, bathrooms, porn theatres, the bookstores, shoplifting, jumping from job to job. I wasn't going to commit suicide because I thought that for sure would be a one-way ticket to hell, but I sure wasn't going to pass up a free ride out of here.

 Eventually, Falexis had been kicked out of the shelter and she had nowhere to go so I let her come and live with me. Glen's appearances at my place had become more frequent as well. Also, I discovered that Alicia, a large light-skinned, boyish-looking lesbian that I met one-night dancing at the Liberty lived just across the porch from me. Everybody had converged at my apartment for an impromptu party as we got ready to go out to the Liberty.

I decided that if Falexis was going to be living with me she was going to have to carry her own weight. She was not employable accept to work cleaning up at the bathhouse when she was sober enough to concentrate. Drag was the only way she was going to make any money but nobody liked her as a boy or a girl.

It was Sunday night and the Liberty was hoppin. Everyone had come out for the big weekly Sunday night Drag show. All the local popular Big-name Queens performed on Sunday night.

Falexis often tried to get billed on Sunday night but they wouldn't let her go on anymore as she could never really cut the mustard.

Jamie Blue, Aggie Dune, Donna Nicole, Morgan were al in the show lineup tonight, Morgan that night tantalized the audience to the tune of Sexy by Clymaxx. She gyrated around the stage in a black two-piece swimsuit sequined stiletto pumps and a feather boa, periodically accenting the song by pulling feathers from the boa and sexily tossing them at the boys. The audience loved it and they compensated her quite well for the entertainment.

That's when it hit me, when we got home that night I pulled Falexis aside. "Girl did you see Morgan's performance tonight, wasn't it fabulous?"

"Yeah she's so pretty" Falexis half-heartedly replied.

"You know you could make just as much money as her."

"(Snort), what are you talking about, they boo me off the stage every time I get up there."

"All you need is a manager and that manager is me."

"Ok man-a-ger how the heck you gonna make all this as gorgeous as Morgan." He retorted, grabbing at his belly fat.

"You just leave that to me cuz you gone have to be bringin some money up in here if you plan on livin here."

CHAPTER 17

The following day the phone rang. It was my Mother. "How you doing son." She said sullenly. Every time I would talk to my mom I would get this lump in my throat and a sense of panic.

"I'm ok how are you?" I said, trying to deflect the conversation because I did not want to talk about myself. "Oh we're getting settled in slowly we could really use your help, you never really realize how much stuff you have, how are things with you, you going to church anywhere?"

"No Mom, I am not. Just working."

"Well, I was really calling to let you know, had you heard that they set a date for Scheidler's Trial?"

I had totally ignored everything about Weighton Tabernacle and Scheidler, the case, the district attorney. I was trying to enjoy life and forget about all that, but it just would not go AWAY!

"No mom I hadn't heard anything."

"Well they called us and they set the date so we will be flying in to be there for you."

"Ok."

"Are you nervous about that?"

"No," I said apathetically

"Well, I want to warn you too, that the people you might think are your friends may not be anymore so, until it is over, don't trust anyone with information about what is going on with the case. Ok?"

"Ok"

"Well that's what I needed to let you know, everything's ok though right?, you know your mother worries."

"Yes I know, I mean, everything is fine mom"

"Well do stay in touch I really miss you."

"Ok, I will, Bye."

"Bye-bye son."

 I lied, the landlord had already been by beating on my door twice this month and I had already been hauled into court on an eviction notice last month that thankfully I was able to beat since I brought the past due rent to court with me but, Que Sera Sera as Hakuna Matata wasn't around yet.

I was only working sporadically so I was putting my eggs in a very questionable basket named Falexis.

 It was Wednesday night again and it was time for me to unleash my plan. I put Falexis in a one piece black bathing suit and a pair of black sneakers that I had adorned with a glue gun and small balls of tin foil. I made her a boa out of old washcloths and stuffed her chest with pillow fuzz. We kept the taped glasses and messy hair. I queued the

DJ to strike up Sexxy by Climaxx and Falexis burst from behind the curtain in a parody of Morgan's Sunday night performance.

She looked a hot mess, but it was hysterical as Falexis jumped around on stage making all of Morgan's sexy moves appear as unattractive as possible. Falexis thrust her hips about like she was one of the lollipop kids from the Wizard of OZ and pulling the pillow fuzz from her bustier and tossing it at the boys. They loved it! So much so they went into their pockets for Falexsis tonight. She even got through a repeat of the latter half of the song to give her more time and more dollars. We came home with about 180 dollars of which I of course immediately budgeted for expenses.

Falexsis loved the attention and I loved the money so next week we would work even harder. I heard Morgan was not so pleased, but so what, she was the star we were the late-night comedians, and when you are in the public eye nothing is sacred. Besides we might have a new target next week.

 When Glen, Falexsis, Alicia, and I came home from the club I was plastered. When I came through the door I tripped and fell in the kitchen. I was laughing so hard I couldn't get up. They were all trying to help me up when there was a knock at the door.

"What the hell?" I said, getting myself up from the floor. I went to the door and looked out the window. I couldn't quite make out the short smiling figure outside the door. Then everything seemed to slow down and my heart swelled up like a balloon when I realized it was Rick Cordonowski. Rick was the buff little all-star jock from Weighton Tabernacle School who always was a part of my nighttime fantasies growing up. Since I had moved, we now lived just blocks away from each other.

While he was still a student he coached our JV basketball team on which I unskillfully played just to be around him and look at his body. I fantasized about him so much because I thought he was so fine that I would never have a chance with him. Now, here he was on my doorstep unannounced just looking as tempting as ever. All the other occupants of the house were gazing at him too as we talked in the kitchen.

I sent everyone into the living room so we could talk. We reminisced about our days at Weighton Tabernacle School and youth group.

"Can I see your bedroom?" Rick just blurted out.

"Yeah, you can see my bedroom." My heart started to race as I could hear ogling and giggles coming from the living room.

Rick and I sat privately in my bedroom for awhile talking and looking at old yearbooks that I still had. We talked about school and church, Scheidler too. When we talked about Scheidler my mother's voice started ringing in my head from our phone conversation when she said not to trust anyone until the case was over. It was about then when Rick said he wanted to know what it would be like to be with another guy. and that was why he was here at my house. He said he thought it would be best for his first time to do it with somebody he knew.

"What do you think?" He asked. Mom's voice was quickly silenced.

Rick stood up and pulled his shirt off and I just watched intently I mean, this was what had dreamed about nearly every night of my adolescent life. His shorts now. I was frozen except for the swivel of my tongue pulling my bottom lip between my teeth. But my frigidity melted away quickly when he stood in front of me totally naked. I quickly joined him, I turned out the lights and Rick and I were making my dream come true. It wasn't the first time I had seen Rick naked but it was the first time I got to be this close, touch, taste. He stayed the night too, so I got to hold him close to me all night, which felt really fuckin good.

The next morning Rick awoke in a frenzy scurrying about and pulling his clothes on and said,

"Shit, I was supposed to be home hours ago!" Wiping the sleep from my eyes and love-struck I just watched him dress his well-formed body and said,

"Maybe we could get together this weekend or something."

"Yeah, that'd be cool."

I walked Rick to the door and watched as he sprinted down the steps.

Falexis and Alicia emerged from the living room grinning from ear to ear.

"Girl, don't you have an apartment next door why are you still here?" I scowled.

"So how was it?" Falexis asked.

"How was what? We were just talking."

"Well, I wanna learn that language honey!" Alicia said. Alicia and Falexis both laughed out their noses

"OUT!" I playfully demanded.

"Bye, ooh yess Ferron ooh yess!" Alicia howled as she went across the porch to her apartment.

"Shut, up?"

In hindsight. My mother probably wasn't off track about her warning. Rick had a strange connection to Scheidler as well. Rick was always doing some kind of errand for Scheidler for which he got paid. Rick had never shown any kind of sexual interest in me before and here he was throwing himself at me so close to the trial? Had Scheidler sent him to my apartment to get information or worse take me out before I could testify. Had Falexis and Alicia's presence at my apartment that night saved my life?

It's Friday Night and Tara's was pretty full. It was unusually festive in there and more black folks than usual too. Just then, this short funny looking man wearing some kind of pimp hat approached me. It was not the kind of pimp hat from the early seventies mind you, but one you might see older men wear, almost derby like. He wore glasses and had a certain "you know you want me" air about him. I was not impressed however. Nevertheless, I was not one to be rude so when he struck up a conversation with me I returned the gesture. His name was

"Erol, Erol Graymond," he said, and people affectionately or non-affectionately referred to him as just Graymond

I called him Erol. Erol would always load up the jukebox with every Donna Summer song it contained and jump up to dance every time she came on. Erol loved Donna Summer so much he would threaten bodily harm to anyone who spoke an ill word of her. He was a character, to say the least.

To this day discrepancies remain between us as to the events that transpired in the way we met. He says I hit on him, which I absolutely know did not occur. Erol was often full of himself and he would assume fabricate an entire evening than allow the mere notion of a man rejecting his self-perceived smooth advances to be entered into any gay historical archives.

Erol drove me home that night. On the way, he would beep his horn at virtually every guy on the street we passed. He would slow the car down to get a good look at them or see if he was getting any play from them.

"Do you know these guys or something?" I asked

"Naw man, I am just looking to see who might be trade."

"Trade?"

"You don't know what trade is?"

"No, should I?"

"Trade is those guys who mess around, they don't look or act gay, mmm real men, you might could get em into bed if you get em what they want. liquor, weed, coke., hell a warm bed. Somethin in trade for the sex."

"Oh."

"Thing about it is the sex is pretty decent most of the time and you don't really have to worry about them whinin or wantin to fall in love and shit."

We pulled in to my parking lot and Erol came up to the apartment. I guess he thought he was coming up for some sex but that, wasn't going to happen. I just didn't like him that way. We had a cocktail and talked for a while as he enlightened me on many aspects of gay life that I was yet unaware of. Then he shuffled off home, or wherever he went.

Falexis didn't come home that night. I was worried about her. In fact, I didn't see Falexis for several weeks. Since I wasn't working and Falexis was missing in action not much money was coming in and It wasn't long before another eviction notice was on the door.

The time was also approaching for me that I would have to testify in Scheidler's trial. My parents were coming to town for the trial and it was going to be apparent to them that I had failed miserably living on my own.

Erol came by to see if I wanted to go out. He could see that I was going out of my mind. Erol lived in Fairport with his Aunt and Uncle so I thought I felt a little kinship with him being a suburban boy, but Erol was no suburban boy he just lived with his Auntie in the suburbs. Erol often talked about how he was getting tired of living with them and was looking for the first opportunity to get out. I told him what was going on with me too and in the course of our conversation, we had agreed to try and put whatever money we had into finding a place together. I jumped at the opportunity just so I could tell my parents everything was fine.

Nevertheless, the day finally came. Ironically the day I was to testify in Scheidler's trial was the same day I was on the docket in the same building to be evicted from my first apartment. The Scheidler case was not all that dramatic. I did not get to use any of the lines I had put to memory from every episode of L.A Law I had watched. My parents due to formality were not allowed in the courtroom while I testified. I guess it was to prevent any coaching.

All I had to do was answer yes or no to the questions and point the long finger of identification when they asked if the man that did these things to me was in this courtroom today? I thought about falling out of my seat on the stand in tears screaming "It was him your honor.. hiiim!" just for the drama, but then I thought, "I just want this to be over." Then, it was over.

I left the stand and bolted for the elevator trying to make it to the courtroom downstairs where my eviction proceedings were being held but apparently, that was over too.

"Oh well." I thought and made my way back upstairs. The Scheidler case had become so much larger than just me that I felt disconnected from the outcomes now, and that my part in it seemed so insignificant. It wasn't about me anymore. I was just another statistic. Everyone kept hugging on me seeming to be concerned for my emotional well being, but I pretty much felt nothing. I just let them carry on so they could feel better about themselves. But it was over. Sheidler was found guilty on all counts but somehow his sentence seemed lenient. All I remember hearing was he got like 8 years but it was chopped down to like 3 or 4. I didn't even care anymore. I was just so angry that I had to spend any more time on this. I just didn't even want to deal with it. I stuffed those feelings in the same place I stuffed all the rest of my pain and sealed it over with a good meal.

CHAPTER 18

Mom and Dad flew back to California a few days later and I was left with the business of trying to get moved in somewhere with Erol before the Marshal came to put me out of my apartment. Erol and I managed to find a studio apartment down on South Clinton Avenue. It was in the hood but it didn't matter to me I just didn't want to be on the street. Erol loved it because it gave him unlimited access to trade.

The apartment was one room and it had a couch that could convert into two single beds. It was roach-infested and the kitchen was so small when you turned around you were back in the living room. I am sure it was under four hundred dollars at the time and we could barely afford it even between the two of us. Somehow we made it work month to month.

For the most part, we got along pretty well. Erol had the most insane sense of humor. Despite the fact he had no hair on his head he could daily be seen exiting the bathroom with his head wrapped in a bath towel piled high as if he had the last locks on earth.

We had a pretty good time together other than when Erol was having his unmedicated manic depressive moments. This is when he hated the world, everyone and everything in it. The never-ending rants and ravings of this dissatisfied lady of the house who would measure the remains of his carton of Dole-Pine-Orange-Banana juice with a magic marker just to make sure no one was drinking it, began to grate heavily on my last black nerve.

Then it would be over again, and he would be asking if I would join him for a night out on the town.

"It's Monday night, You wanna go to the pub?"

"Erol it's already one am and it is a Monday night. Nothing is happening on a Monday."

"C'mon we won't stay out late, I just wanna see what's going on."

I knew if he went out alone he would just get into trouble so I slipped on some shorts and a tee shirt and waited for him at the car. Erol came outside finally and was headed to the car.

Damn, what took you so long girl, after all that time you should be coming out here dripping gold dust!" I said flippantly.

When he came into the light I felt my face making an expression of shock. Erol had on a pair of holey yellow skin tight gym shorts that looked like he had since sixth grade, a too-tight tank top and some flip flops. His shorts were so tight you could see the imprint of his dick.

I just looked at him and shook my head.

"What?!" he said. "We must not be going very far cuz all you need is a corner to stand on!"

"Don't hate." He said popping his fingers.

When we got to the Pub it was just as I expected, empty. Erol ordered us a couple of drinks and we started to just feel the music all by ourselves. Soon we were dancing on the dance floor having a grand ol' time, just actin a fool. It wasn't long before we felt taps on our shoulders and the bars security staff was asking us to leave. Erol's mood swings would often throw me off. I couldn't tell sometimes if he was really angry, or if he was just being dramatic and silly.

However tonight Erol's demeanor in combination with the liquor turned into both drama and anger and of course, he went into one of his rants. Standing there with his hand on his hip and one finger in the security guard's face.

"WHAT?! You're throwing ME OUT, ME!? I will have you KNOW, that I spend more money up in here than you make in a WEEK and you have the au-dac-i-ty to throw ME, Out?! You CAN'T say we were disturbing any CUSTOMERS cuz ya ain't GOT NO FUCKIN CUSTOMERS BUT US" I just stood there laughing with my hands over my face for a moment taking the whole scene in.

Erol dressed like he ain't got no sense, cussin out the staff and about to get the police called on us..ah hell naw, jokes over, time to go. I am not going to jail tonight not when I could have been in the bed sleep.

"C'mon Erol let it go they want us to leave." "No, Not until I've had my satisfaction!"

"We're leaving Erol." I took Erol by the arm. "You better be glad he is here to hold me back! And BELIEVE ME, this is NOT over YET!" he yelled as we went out of the door.

"Nigga, you crazy!"

"I know, but how they just gonna put us out like that?" "Could it be you look like a stank ho?"

"Uh excuse me? I do not care what I have on, I ALWAYS look good."

"Umm..ok, Boy lets go I have to work tomorrow."

I decided to drive us home since Erol was still feeling himself. On the way back Erol spotted some boys he thought were trade.

"Slow down slow down, you drive to fast I can't see!" Erol said as he tried to reach over and beep the horn.

"Can I do this please?" I said. I glanced to my right and I saw Falexis walking down the street looking dirty and pretty tore up.

"There go that old nasty queen you let live with you," Erol said. I just kept driving, but inside myself, I said, "God please don't ever let that happen to me."

We eventually made it home and just went to bed despite Erol's attempts to bring strangers over to keep the party goin.

CHAPTER 19

I went to the Liberty early Friday night. I was feeling lonely, depressed, and disgusted. I hadn't had any male attention in several weeks and I was beginning to go through withdrawals. Rick Cordonowski had made no attempts to get back in touch with me and it seemed when I tried to find him, he was intentionally MIA. There I stood at my traditional post staring into the video screen embedded in the table shedding tears in my beer. I was drinking beer because tonight, I could not afford my usual Bacardi 151 and cokes with the lime and cherry twists.

I was standing strategically parallel to the stage and facing the front door of the club. This way I could survey the entire establishment. I could see who came in, more importantly, who was leaving and if they were alone. I could also still be entertained by the stage show and whatever was going on at the bar.

Nikki, was a very pretty rather feminine Sade looking kind of guy. He was a great dancer and always had a very in-your-face dominatrix flair to his personality. He never really dressed in what I described as full drag, but he always looked great. Nikki never really considered himself a drag queen, he still wore a lot of makeup, but never dresses so much. A lot of the gurlz back then did drag to make a living. Nikki however had a job he went to most days. Tonight though, I guess Nikki felt that the entertainment at the Liberty had waxed old and he needed to liven it up a bit.

The lights over the stage began to flash and the speakers started to bump Jody Watley's, Real Love and Nikki finger popped his way onto the stage with his hair pulled back in a moving ponytail, flawless makeup, huge hoop earrings, a cut off embroidered denim jacket, and fashionably clashed the whole ensemble with a ballerina styled tutu, and some hot leather hip boots. That outfit was fuckin hot! The crowd immediately jumped to their feet and howled their praises for Nikki and his fashion sense giving their many dollars to back it up. When the song finished the crowd screamed and applauded as the sounds of the next dance number filled the room. Everyone hit the floor in excitement. It was then that Nikki came around the corner from backstage and was headed for the bar when he noticed me standing there crying in my beer.

"Gurl, what are you standin ova here lookin all pitiful for?"

"I'm just having a rough night." I muttered.

"Aw, what's the matter did your mamma or your lover die or something?" Nikki said with concern in his eyes.

"Well I guess I could be a little homesick but, I never had a lover for him to die or anything, in fact, it doesn't seem like anybody wants me," I said woefully.

Nikki's face dropped from concern to an unsympathetic stare.

"Chyle, I am giving you three seconds to get all the way over it 1, 2, 3, there, you're done." he said waving his arms like he was Endora from Bewitched

I just looked at him.

"I just keep thinking what is the point of being out here night after night or even being gay if don't nobody want you?" I said,

"Honey, how old are you?"

"Eighteen"

"O my dear Jesus, honey you really do need to get over it. Don't you realize you have a whole lifetime ahead of you to deal with depression and rejection and self-loathing?" He said grabbing my hand. "Now come on let's Dance!, Cuz now, is the time for DAHNCING!,"

Nikki and I were dancing it seemed all night when just then almost seamlessly, I was dancing with someone new. I don't know, I guess he had been eyeing me all night and he had just decided to move in. David and I finished the night out dancing together and, he was buying my drinks.

He wasn't exactly the prettiest button on the shirt, in fact, I didn't even really get a good look at him until we were outside the club. I was just enjoying the vibe and the good feeling I was having holding on to him while we danced, from all the attention he was giving me.

David was a short dark-skinned brotha, that kinda put you in the mind of Gary Coleman. He had a little more sugar in his tank than black gay men say they prefer by the segregated standards of the day, but back then I had not learned of all those ignorant black gay social morays we so vehemently employ against each other. To me, David was a really sweet guy who seemed to really like me, and that was enough for me. From that night on David and I grew to be lovers and he assumed the title of, my first real boyfriend. He was someone who wanted to be with me as much as I wanted to be with him.

David and I spent a lot of time together when we could. Sometimes he would stay over at the apartment with Erol and me and go to work from there. Erol was dating a guy named Ron at the time so sometimes it would get pretty crowded and noisy at night in that studio apartment with all the side by side lovemaking, but we managed.

David took good care of me. He would cook dinners and cuddle and comfort me at night and always made sure I lacked for nothing sexually. He always made sure to give me some bomb ass head before he left for work in the morning. David nor I had a car so we commuted everywhere on the bus. Since I got off later than he did, David would make the extra sacrifice to catch the bus out to my job on the other side of town to meet me. He called himself coming to pick me up so we could ride home together. It was only in hindsight that I was able to see how sweet and special that was.

Sometimes we would stop at a nice restaurant and have dinner before going back to the apartment. We'd talk about our day, laugh about the craziness in our respective lives and we even hinted around making plans to live together to alleviate that stressor. I had a really good one on my hands, but I was much too young and inexperienced to recognize it. If things were different I probably would have held on to David forever.

Well, I managed to get a job at Schatz Stationers as an Assistant to the Assistant manager. I was a key holder. I was often responsible for opening and closing the store. My relationship with my boss however was very antagonistic. Nan, my boss, seemed to be the kind of woman who needed a great deal of validation in her life and sought it out by annoying the hell out of everyone else around her. I would often hear her going on and on in tears on the phone with a friend of hers about her out of control sons and how her husband had done her so wrong and left her. At times I really believed that she was taking those issues out on me.

I was on to close the store on Friday and it was also my weekend off so David and I had planned to spend some time together. When I got home I reached in my pocket and found a twenty-dollar bill. I was puzzled by this because I did not recall having it earlier. Then it hit me. "SHIT!" Earlier that day one of the cashiers had asked me to make change. I got distracted and did not place the twenty dollars back in the safe. Now the safe was going to be short. I thought to myself. I called the store knowing that it was closed but I left a message for the opening manager about the twenty dollars.

That morning apparently the opening manager did not even count the safe nor did they check the messages or else he would have been aware of the shortage. I didn't receive a return phone call so I called again and spoke to Nan.

"Nan, was the safe short today?" "I don't know we'll have to count it." "OK, count it and let me know because I have twenty dollars that I found in my pocket that I can't account for where it came from, if the safe is short I will bring it back up there today."

When she came back to the phone she affirmed that the safe was short. So I told her I was on my way. I asked Erol if he could drive me out there because the bus was gonna take forever on a Saturday. When I walked into the office, I handed Nan the twenty dollars and she said. "I will need your keys and your badge as well."

"Why?"

"You are being terminated for policy violation."

"Nan are you off your meds again? It was an honest mistake!" I snapped.

"No monies are to leave this store without being properly accounted for, and are in a locked bank deposit bag, your keys, and your badge please."

I could feel my whole face numbing and turning to poison. I removed the keys and my badge from my key ring and dropped them tauntingly on her desk. As I turned to leave I said.

"Thank you, Nan, for this opportunity to work for Schatz Stationers, I do hope in the future you are able to one day secure a faithful husband and finally produce some decent children."

As I turned to walk out I could hear the rolling of Nan's chair and her screaming

"Yoou BITCH!" Suddenly I felt her body thrust against my back and her arms around my neck as she lunged at me. We tussled scuffled and boxed on the stock room floor until security arrived and separated the two of us. I just stood there calmly while Nan kept raving on and trying to get at me as if she were on an episode of Jerry Springer. Shonda, one of the black girls who worked in the store was able to corroborate my story of how Nan attacked me first and the security guard asked me if I wanted to press charges. I was supposed to meet David very soon so I wasn't going to waste any more time on her. I was worried though, I was worried about how I was going to survive I did not want to end up on the streets. Not like Falexis.

So what does a young gay black man do when his back is against the wall and he has no options? He sucks it up and calls Momma and Daddy.

When the usual battery of questions came out I just told the truth. Things were not going well and I didn't think I was going to make it much longer here in Rochester. A few moments later Mom called me back and told me it just so happened that Dad was coming to Rochester on business in a few weeks and he had arranged a ticket for me to fly back to California with him.

"Fuck!" I said to myself.

CHAPTER 20

I met with Glen one night for drinks to tell him I was leaving and I went over to David's house to tell him later that week. I didn't tell Erol, I didn't know how to. I felt bad because I was going to be leaving him in an already bad situation and it was at a time when Erol was on one of his tirades, so we weren't really speaking much anyway. As time went on however he started noticing that my things around the apartment were becoming more and more scarce as I was packing them away.

I walked into the apartment the day that I was going to meet Mrs. Lawson. I was going to stay with the Lawson's for a few days until Dad came to get me. Erol was on the phone with someone, and I overheard him say "I think he is moving out on me." I grabbed the things that I had stuffed into a garbage bag and started for the door.

"You're not going to say anything?" Erol said.

"Erol I am really sorry things did not work out the way we planned, but my ride is here to pick me up. I am flying to California with my Dad next week."

"You're sorry? That is something I already know, I know you're sorry, now apologize!" Erol spewed.

"Erol I said I was sorry, there is nothing else I can do."

"Exactly, there is nothing anybody ever, can do."

"I gotta go man, she's waiting." I went out the door and got in the car with Mrs. Lawson and we drove to her house where I would be staying until Dad arrived in a few days.

A few days later when Dad arrived, he brought some suitcases for me to put my stuff in. When we were getting ready to leave Mrs. Lawson came from the back of the house, from the room where I was staying, calling to me.

"Ferron? Ferron?"

"Yes?"

"I was doing some cleaning up and checking to make sure you had everything and I found this, is this yours?" My face went blank and I froze, as in her hand was a size 14 mother of pearl pump. A ladies' shoe that I had worn in an attempt to revive Tramaine one night at the club to try and raise some rent money. Somehow the shoe had made it in with my fevered packing.

"Nnoo.. that's not mine," I said blinking and with as straight a face as I could manage.

"Well, I just wondered, because I had not seen it before and I know it's not mine I can't wear this size."

"No ma'am it isn't mine."

"Hmm, I wonder where it came from?

"Couldn't tell ya." I said,

She hugged me goodbye and said, "You take care of yourself and stay out of trouble ok?"

"I will.. Bu-Bye."

It was Friday night and I was sharing a bed with My Dad in a Hotel Room. Eew! I couldn't go out like this! We were actually staying at a hotel that wasn't far from Tara's and the Liberty so, I put on some clothes and decided to have one last hurrah before I left for good. I stepped into Tara's and tried to mingle a bit but the feel wasn't right. It was usually Erol and me cracking jokes on everybody who walked by.

I went into the restroom, I don't know, I guess just to see what I could see. When I came out Erol was at the bar ordering a drink. I went over to him to tried and make peace. I tapped him on the shoulder and he turned, grinning that grin he would grin when he was going to meet a new man. When his eyes hit me his grin dropped.

"Oh, its you." He said turning his face away from me.

"Erol man I am really sorry ok?" The bartender set Erol's drink on the counter. He picked it up and before I could get another word out, Erol threw the drink in my face. "Rum and coke is your favorite, right?!" Apparently, he ran out of the bar right after that because by the time I cleared my eyes he was gone. My white stonewash pattern shirt was ruined, catty queens were laughing and pointing fingers. I was humiliated. I just left the bar, went back to the hotel, and slithered back into bed with my Dad.

This is how it would end for me in Rochester. It was all ok though, I would begin anew all the way on the other side of the country come Monday. Where nobody knew who I was. It was another chance to rewrite my life. This time I know things are going to be better.

Made in the USA
Middletown, DE
17 January 2023

21540215R00083